MY SAM JOHNSON

MY SAM JOHNSON

A BIOGRAPHY FOR GENERAL READERS

WAYNE JONES

WILLIAM & PARK

William & Park, Ottawa, Ontario, Canada
williamapark.com

ISBN: 978-1-7388960-0-4 (paperback)
ISBN: 978-1-7388960-1-1 (ebook)
ISBN: 978-1-7388960-2-8 (audiobook)

Published 2023

Cover photo: *Samuel Johnson*, 2013, original painting by artist Bunny Glue (Anna Bernhardt), after *Johnson Arguing*, 1769, by Joshua Reynolds

Names: Jones, Wayne, 1959- author.
Title: My Sam Johnson : a biography for general readers / Wayne Jones.
Description: Ottawa, Ontario, Canada : William & Park, [2023] |
                 Includes bibliographical references and index.
Identifiers: ISBN: 978-1-7388960-0-4 (paperback) | 978-1-7388960-1-1 (ebook) | 978-1-7388960-2-8 (audiobook)
Subjects: LCSH: Johnson, Samuel, 1709-1784. | Authors, English--18th century--Biography. | LCGFT: Biographies.
Classification: LCC: PR3533 .J66 2023 | DDC: 828.609--dc23

for my mother
Maxine Jones
with much love and gratitude

the night cometh
John 9:4

(English translation of the Greek inscription on the face of Sam's watch)

CONTENTS

PHOTOS AND ILLUSTRATIONS

YOU CAN FIND MANY PHOTOS related to Sam which I took during several trips to England, as well as illustrations which I commissioned specifically for the book. They are available at **MySamJohnson.com**, as well as on Instagram **@mysamjohnson**.

On the book site you can also find links to a blog and podcast that I maintained during the writing of the book.

This book contains two illustrations, one on page 92 showing the use of the long *s*, and one on page 131 showing the itinerary of the trip to the Scottish Hebrides that Sam and James Boswell took in 1773.

PREFACE

THIS IS A BOOK ABOUT a writer who was born over three hundred years ago, but I am still as fascinated by him as I was forty years ago when I was introduced to his work at university.

Samuel Johnson—*Sam*—seems very much alive to me. Most other people have either never heard of him. Or they have read about him in the famous biography by James Boswell: Sam as the irascible but wise old man, or "Dr. Johnson." They might know the anecdotes and the famous quotes, and even though overall they do have a kind of picture of Sam, it's a little skewed. Boswell's biography, for one thing, is notoriously uneven, and covers only the last third or so of Sam's life in any detail. They didn't meet until Sam was fifty-three, and they spent only 426 days together in total over the course of twenty-one years. Scholars know Sam of course. As with all literary figures who are studied in universities, Sam's popularity has waned and then recovered. Perhaps the only eighteenth-century writers who compete for equivalent stature are Alexander Pope and Jonathan Swift.

There are many reasons why a person might be interested in a particular author. The obvious one is the writing, either the style of it or the content. The distinction is important and illustrative. For some readers, style—not in the narrow sense of personal quirkiness, but referring to skill with language, the ability to express, to achieve the right tone, to *write*—style is the only thing that matters. In apologizing for his editing of the transcript of an interview, Vladimir Nabokov, often cited as one of the best English prose stylists of the twentieth (or any) century, said in a letter to Robert Hughes, an interviewer for National Educational Television: "I am terribly sorry if my extensive cuts are causing you any disappointment, but I am sure you will understand that after all I am almost exclusively a writer, and my style is all I have."

For other readers it is not the style but the content or subject matter of the writing that is important, and for still others it is simply the author's life that interests them. They may like an author because of his biography, his life story. Perhaps they identify with his struggle from obscurity and his success in overcoming hardships in order to become a successful writer. Or perhaps his life has been quite an adventure and they like a good tale.

I am interested in Sam for those and many other reasons.

I first met Sam during one of the courses I took at Memorial University in St. John's, Newfoundland, Canada, as part of my Bachelor of Arts (Honours) studies. It was the eighteenth-century survey course which I took in the fall of 1980 and the winter of 1981. The teacher, Patrick O'Flaherty, was passionate about the eighteenth century and about Sam in particular. An article that O'Flaherty published in 1978 influenced me in my choice of topic for my master's thesis at the University of Toronto during 1981–1982. In the article O'Flaherty argues that there is a "lack of any readily perceived symmetry" in a series of essays which Sam published in 1750–1752 called the *Rambler*, and that assertion always stuck with me—because I disagreed with it strongly. I took "symmetry" to mean "organization," and I knew even then that though the rhetorical method in Sam's *Rambler* essays was not neat and orderly—not *symmetrical*—yet they were very well organized. I argued in my thesis that there is always a "coherent organization," writing: "A *Rambler* essay is not logically or symmetrically structured around some central thesis. Rather, it progresses from paragraph to paragraph, from idea to idea, from event to event in a manner which may sometimes be abrupt but is always coherent."

But this book is not about or for me. It is, as the subtitle implies, for those who know a little or nothing at all about Sam Johnson and would like to know more. It is not for the scholar, but for the general reader.

ACKNOWLEDGEMENTS AND THANKS

I WOULD LIKE TO THANK the following people for agreeing to be interviewed for this book and for providing me with their expertise, knowledge, and informed opinion about a wide variety of topics related to Sam and to life in eighteenth-century England. I carried out interviews in 2019 and 2020, mostly by telephone or in person, but also by email or direct messaging, with the following people:

Katie Barclay	Patrick O'Flaherty
David Benson	Laura J. Rosenthal
George Boulukos	Annette Rubery
Stephanie Clayton	William Savage
Colleen Cotter	Rebecca Shapiro
Frans De Bruyn	Tiffany Stern
Richard Gorrie	Robert St-Louis
Judith Hawley	Tony Thorne
Jonathan Hyde	Scott Turner
Kathleen Lubey	Helen Williams
Frank Lynch	Joanne Wilson

Many thanks to Carleton University's MacOdrum Library in Ottawa, Canada, for access to resources both in print and online that were conveniently available in the writing of this book. Thanks also to the staff I met at the Samuel Johnson Birthplace Museum in Lichfield, Staffordshire (Joanne Wilson and Penny Taylor) and at Dr Johnson's House in London (Celine McDaid). I appreciate the kindness and encouragement of the Johnson Society (Lichfield), notably from council members John Winterton and Annette Rubery.

Special thanks to Scott Turner for reading some of Sam's writing and providing me with comments on the challenges in understanding it.

I appreciate the enthusiastic and helpful comments from people who responded to the "Your Sam Johnson" section of my website for the book: Barbara Baker, Paul Buttle, Judith Hazlett, Lona Manning, Celine McDaid, Bruce Meyer, Julie Murray, Rosemary O'Neill, Hugh Reid, Adam Stevenson, and John A. Vance.

Warm gratitude to my editor, Jennia D'Lima, who was not only rigorous, meticulous, and comprehensive, but also a pleasure to work with.

Thanks to Dave Jones and Judith Hazlett for their suggestions to improve the book.

On the audiobook side, I love the narration that Veronica Saretsky provided. It hits all the right notes, literally and figuratively.

Thanks, Jennifer Malisauskas and Kris Laptos, of Lapbaby Designs for the beautiful website they designed for the book (MySamJohnson.com).

Thank you, David and Manon Wogahn, for your expertise, diligence, and kindness.

Finally, I would like to thank Marjorie Doyle, the widow of Patrick O'Flaherty (1939–2017). It was Patrick who so enthusiastically introduced me to Sam during those classes at Memorial University in the early 1980's. Marjorie was kind enough to share some details about Patrick, saying that he was "a literary man, appreciated great writing, loved words, had a keen sense of humour and irony, loved satire, respected working writers." He loved Jonathan Swift, as anyone does who appreciates great satire. "Patrick was also a passionate, proud, patriotic Newfoundlander, but at the same time Newfoundland disappointed him, past and present." Patrick was, as she accurately put it, "a hard man to sum up—any sentence or two seems reductive ... He was an intellectual but also down to earth and practical. He was a skeptic, but not a cynic ... He was always happy in an archive or library. He was a careful researcher and scholar and exacted of himself and others that ideas be thought out and clearly expressed." Thank you, Marjorie, and thank you, Patrick.

Ottawa, Canada
September 18, 2023

GUILT AND PENANCE

IN THE SMALL TOWN OF Uttoxeter in the West Midlands of England, it is raining hard. Sam Johnson is seventy-two years old and he has made the trip 30 kilometres north from Lichfield, the city of his birth. He doesn't live in either place now. Since he set out from Lichfield for London when he was twenty-seven, he has mostly lived in the big city, but he still visits his home town, partly out of duty and partly out of desire to see family and friends who still live there.

On this trip to Lichfield in the fall of 1781 he leaves for a day though and goes to Uttoxeter for a very specific purpose. This year is the fiftieth anniversary of the death of his father Michael, who worked as a bookseller in Lichfield. Like other booksellers and men in other trades, he couldn't make a decent living simply by staying in the town where his business was located. And so he occasionally travelled to Uttoxeter, known as a "market town" because it opened up the market square to tradespeople in the area to set up stalls to sell their various wares.

Sam also remembers that one day when he was a teen-ager he said no when his father asked him to come with him to Uttoxeter to help out at the stall on a market day. Now fifty years later the memory is still sharp and he feels compelled to do something to make up for his past disobedience. He feels some sympathy for the father whom he reluctantly helped most of the time, but not always.

And so he just stands in the rain right at the spot where his father used to set up his stall.

"I was disobedient," he acknowledges later. "I refused to attend my father to Uttoxeter-market. Pride was the source of that refusal, and the remembrance of it was painful."

Painful is a strong word for the memory of an event—and arguably a minor event, something any son might do—that happened so long before. But no. Sam remembers it after all those years and wants to make up for it somehow.

"I desired to atone for this fault; I went to Uttoxeter in very bad weather, and stood for a considerable time bareheaded in the rain, on the spot where my father's stall used to stand. In contrition I stood, and I hope the penance was expiatory."

This single incident in Sam's life provides almost a full display of all the most important things you need to know in order to understand his life and his char-acter. First, there is regret for something he has done (or not done) and an effort to make up for it somehow.

Guilt and penance. He embodied those characteristics throughout his entire life, annually looking back at what he had failed to accomplish and at how much time he had wasted, and then both praying to God for forgiveness and promising that he would try to do better in the new year. The unadorned self-criticism (even self-flagellation) is sometimes hard to read. You have sympathy for a man who is being so relentlessly harsh with himself. There is nothing of the tone of the New Year's resolutions that many people make each year—lose weight, read more, be nicer to people—but rather Sam's resolutions were extremely negative and self-critical. He considered himself a failure even during those years when he had been very productive, writing long articles or essays twice a week, planning a dictionary, publishing an edition of the plays of Shakespeare with a full set of notes and comments. It didn't matter: he had not done enough, he wasted time, he begged his Creator for forgiveness, and he asked for strength to do better in the future.

Another important thing to note about his standing in the rain is the time frame. He was a teenager who refused to get out of bed and go help his father, but *fifty years later* he still remembers it. This implies that it isn't something that occurred to him just because it happened to be the anniversary of his father's death, but that all those years, somewhere in the back of his mind, it had bothered him. Try to imagine the kind of character and the disposition toward guilt that would cause such a relatively insignificant refusal to stay lodged in his subconscious for such a long time. Many people have done things as bad or worse in their youth, and some of these things they don't even remember, let alone be tortured by guilt about them a half-century later. He never forgives himself.

A third thing to notice about this incident in Uttoxeter is what it says about Sam's troubled history with his immediate family. He spent a year studying at Oxford University but had to return home when the money ran out, and he resented the prospect of having to do work similar to his father's for a living. He was more cut out for teaching or writing and not for regular labour. His father, who was not only a tradesman but also a very poor businessman, was the epitome of what Sam didn't want to be.

His father died in 1731 when Sam was just 22, but his mother lived on in Lichfield. Sam moved to London in 1737 and in the twenty or so years that he was there while his mother was in Lichfield, he visited her infrequently for three years (partly because he couldn't afford to), but after that never visited at all. This was the cause of a lot of guilt for him. He was not there for his mother's death and burial. In fact, after his last trip to see her in 1740, he never even returned to Lichfield for the next twenty-two years, about three years after her death.

As for his brother Nathaniel, about three years younger than Sam, he seems to have had the opposite experience of Sam regarding the family business. Nathaniel not only participated in the bookselling, but actually tried to set up a small branch of the shop in Burton-upon-Trent, a town about 20 km northeast of Lichfield. But something happened. In a letter to his mother in 1735 or 1736, he mentions that he anticipates good success for the shop, but also refers to unspecified crimes "which have given both you & me so much trouble." He tells her that he has given up on the business and partly blames both her and Sam for his failure. She never sent him tools in order to carry it out properly, and he didn't expect much from Sam anyway, who (Nathaniel writes) not only never treated him even with "common civility" when they were both home in Lichfield, but also discouraged their mother from allowing Nathaniel to set up the branch in the first place.

Nathaniel says that his life is going so poorly that he plans to emigrate to Georgia in the United States in two weeks. He never makes it there and in fact he dies in Somerset, a good 250 km southwest of his home. The northern coast of Somerset is on the water, and perhaps Nathaniel made his way there as the first leg in ultimately making his way across the ocean.

He is only twenty-four when he dies, in good health, and some scholars speculate that he may have committed suicide from depression and dissatisfaction over the way his business and life in general were going. His death occurs around the exact day (March 2, 1737) that Sam and David Garrick leave Lichfield to make their careers in London. Very divergent paths, to say the least, for the Johnson brothers.

That incident of standing in the rain at Uttoxeter tells you a few other things about Sam as well. He believes in ritual and symbolism, and during the course of his life this comes through mostly in his religious beliefs. Prayer is a constant activity, notably the ones he composed himself either at the end of a year or on special anniversaries. He makes sure not only to mark these occasions but the content is often self-critical, berating himself for a past year misspent in laziness, or regretting that he wasn't a better person for someone now dead.

Finally, I want to mention an aspect of the incident which will recur often in this book, and that is how Sam talks about it even in his brief description. You get a good hint at least in a small way about what his writing style is like, and frankly how it might be hard to understand at times. Just take the last phrase: "I hope the penance was expiatory." Many years ago when I first read it, I had to pause. "The penance was expiatory." I had to figure out that *the* penance was *his* penance, his standing in the rain, and not some reference to penance in general. And I had to look up *expiatory*. It means atonement or making amends, or, to quote from Sam's own dictionary: "annul[ling] the guilt of a crime by subsequent acts of piety."

This sort of "translation" of Sam's words will sometimes be necessary and I will help the reader try to do it better. The effort is worth it.

CHAPTER 1

BIRTH AND EDUCATION, 1709–1731

NO MATTER HOW BIG WE grow in size, accomplishments, and reputation, we all start as a baby. It's impossible to tell, as we emerge into a less isolated and insulated world, exactly what we will become, how good or bad an influence the people attending our birth will be, and how many years we will be allotted to get something, *anything*, done. The seventy-two-year-old man who stood in the rain at Uttoxeter may have been surprised himself that an event that had happened in his youth still compelled him to enact this apology to his father.

But the nameless baby who will become Samuel Johnson, and mostly call himself Sam, gets his start on September 18, 1709, in the city of Lichfield, in Staffordshire in the West Midlands of England. It is not an easy birth. Sam writes in his autobiographical *Annals*, some fifty-six years later: "My mother had a very difficult and dangerous labour, and was assisted by George Hector, a man-midwife of great reputation. I was born almost dead, and could not cry for some time. When he had me in his arms, he said, 'Here is a brave boy.'" The baby's main ailments are poor eyesight ("almost blind") and scrofula, an inflammation of the lymph nodes of the neck which causes scarring.

The parents are Sarah and Michael Johnson and this is their first child. The scrofula from which Sam suffers is also known as the king's evil. One of the supposed cures is for the person to be touched by the king or queen, and when he is about two and a half years old, during Lent of 1712, his mother takes him to London to be touched by Queen Anne. His mother is pregnant at the time with her second child, Nathaniel, who is born in October.

Michael is a bookseller and Sarah (née Ford) is a mother and housewife, even though she was born of a higher social rank than Michael. They don't get along well. He doesn't like to talk about his business at the end of a day, but his wife is curious about books and asks about them. Neither of them knows the business side of things well, and so Sarah's questions seem like "complaint, fear, and suspicion" to him.

They are poor not so much because of Michael's current daily dealings, but because he took on too many debts too soon and never makes enough money to pay them off and to take care of his family. In 1706 alone, for example, he not only bought a 2,900-volume library, but also rebuilt his house and got married.

Money is not their only problem. The difference in class is a real source of dissension between them—she is from a relatively wealthy family of landowners in

Birmingham, but he is the son of a farm labourer from Cubley (a parish with a population of about a hundred people at the time). Sam goes so far as to describe his mother's attitude toward his father as "contempt," so that she "had no value for his relations."

An aggravating factor is that Michael is "melancholy," what we might call *depressed* these days. Sam confides to a friend later in life—Frances Reynolds, a painter and writer, and sister of the famous painter of the era, Sir Joshua—that Michael suffered from "a morbid disposition of both Body and Mind," which Sam also inherited. It is very real in Sam's case and affects him his whole life. He would have short and long periods that debilitated him, making him unable to work or socialize. (See more about this in the "Digression: Sam's Depression and Harshness with Himself.")

Lichfield itself is a market town in the early eighteenth century, with a population of around three thousand. According to a brief history by the city council, "although there was little industry, the city prospered both from the wealth of the clergy and gentry... and as a thriving coaching city on the main route to the northwest and Ireland." Coaches would stop in Lichfield on their way elsewhere, and a whole service industry of hotels and bars and restaurants emerged to take care of the passengers.

As Sam grows, his early education—learning to read— occurs first at home and at Mrs. Oliver's school for small children. He is about four years old. (The school building doesn't stand any more, but there is a plaque commemorating it in Lichfield.) Sam changes buildings in the usual way, moving on to different schools as his education progresses. He starts to attend Thomas Browne's school when he is about six, and the Lichfield Grammar School about January 1717, when he is seven.

The headmaster at the grammar school, John Hunter, is extremely strict, "wrong-headedly severe," and treats Sam and the other students roughly. Hunter's reasoning for "flogging his boys unmercifully" is "to save you from the gallows." Sam's violations are varied. A fellow student who later went on to become a chief justice describes him as "a lounging boy"—"pass[ing] time indolently or without definite occupation." Or as Sam's own dictionary some forty years later calls it, "living lazily." Another fellow student, and ultimately his life-long friend Edmund Hector, cites Sam's "indolence and procrastination" as irks for Hunter, along with a general tendency for "talking and diverting other boys from their business."

Sam's behaviour—and the fact that he misses nine months of school while he stays with his older cousin Cornelius Ford in Pedmore—are bad enough that in June 1726, when Sam has not yet turned seventeen and is expecting to return to finish off his schooling at Lichfield, Hunter refuses to take him back. The parents scramble but eventually Cornelius arranges to get him admitted into the Stourbridge Grammar School (only about 3 km from Pedmore, and about 45 km southwest of Lichfield).

Alas, Sam is Sam and the problem is not entirely the school or the headmaster. He clashes with the headmaster at Stourbridge as well and *again* is kicked out of school. It's November now and Sam has few options. He is "too old to start at another school" and "too argumentative for the average schoolmaster." The family can't afford to send him to university but he could help out by working with his father in the book business and the parchment factory.

Working in the bookshop bores him but he is in effect "home-schooling" himself with his continued intensive reading. He spends about two years like this, home in Lichfield, working for his father, until an opportunity in the form of a bequest in the will of one of his mother's cousins gives the family some money to be able to send their precocious son to university. The amount is £40 (£6,000 today) and Sam is accepted into Oxford University, residing at Pembroke College, starting in late October 1728. He is nineteen years old when he and his father set out on horseback from Lichfield, a distance of about 135 km southeast. There are several key incidents that will take place at Oxford that define or illustrate his character, establishing his time there as an important part of his development.

On their first night in Oxford, Sam and his father meet William Adams, then a senior fellow and vice-regent of the college (who would later become a friend of Sam's), and William Jorden, who will be Sam's tutor. University really is the logical place for a young man who has done so much reading already. "When I came to Oxford, Dr. Adams, now Master of Pembroke College, told me, I was the best qualified for the University that he had ever known come there."

However, Sam has run-ins with many of his teachers or treats them disrespectfully, just as he has done during his years in school. The very first day after his arrival at Oxford he meets dutifully with Jorden, but then skips the meetings for the next four days: "On the sixth, Mr. Jorden asked me why I had not attended. I answered I had been sliding in Christ-Church meadow. And this I said with as much nonchalance as I am now talking to you. I had no notion that I was wrong or irreverent to my tutor."

At one level this is funny, though a bit surprising that a student would be so bold and forthright with a teacher. Boswell calls it "great fortitude of mind" but Sam later admits it is "stark insensibility" (*insensibility* meaning then what we would now call *insensitivity*). At Oxford just as in many other circumstances throughout his life, there is often this kind of contradictory duality in Sam's behaviour.

Sometimes the duality is in his own head, or is a contradiction between how other people perceive him and what he feels about himself. He appears to some people to be enjoying life at Oxford, but what seems to be happiness on the surface is a mask for inner turmoil.

William Adams says that Sam "was caressed and loved by all about him, was a gay and frolicksome fellow, and passed there the happiest part of his life" (*gay* meant *happy* back then). But in fact at the time Sam is "depressed by poverty, and irritated by disease," and he is compensating for—reacting against—these internal hurts by lashing out externally: "I was mad and violent. It was bitterness which they mistook for frolick. I was miserably poor, and I thought to fight my way by my literature and my wit; so I disregarded all power and all authority."

Being poor is another important circumstance during Sam's life at Oxford, and it is the underlying factor in one of the best-known incidents during his stay there. There is at the time a well-established socio-economic hierarchy among the students, and though Sam is not at the bottom he certainly is nowhere near the top either. In effect they are castes, in descending order:

- **noblemen**: "a small aristocratic group who enjoyed almost unlimited privileges with no need to have a tutor or take a degree. They often dined with the dons, could have pets, luxuriated in splendid private rooms, and generally indulged in a life of debauchery"
- **gentleman commoners**: "the sons of wealthy families [...] with dangerously large amounts of money to spend, proved to be even more notorious in their idleness, drinking, eating and whoring"
- **commoners**: the largest group of students, which includes Sam

- **battelers**: they "had to feed and take care of themselves in return for a reduction of fees"
- **servitors**: "they had to perform certain duties in college, many of them quite menial and degrading, such as waiting on the gentlemen commoners and commoners in hall"

And so there is the incident of the shoes.

Sam thinks highly of the lectures by a tutor in a different college (Christ Church, not Pembroke), and so visits his friend there to hear about the lectures second-hand. But he is embarrassed when he realizes that the students at Christ Church have noticed that his shoes are so worn out that his feet stick through the ends, and when someone leaves a new pair at his door, Sam "threw them away with indignation." He is poor, and sometimes doesn't think about how it looks on the outside, but is angry when he is reminded.

Another duality also manifests itself at Oxford that is in fact a common dynamic with Sam during his whole life: claiming to be lazy and chastising himself for wasting time, while in reality he generally accomplishes an enormous amount. Boswell tries to explain the discrepancy as Sam comparing himself not to what other students read, but to the "vast portion of study which is possible" *at all*, and which very few scholars ever accomplish.

There is ultimately bad practical news for Sam: the money from his aunt's bequest is not enough to fund much more than a year of his attendance at Oxford, and he has to quit university and return home to Lichfield, around December 12, 1729. It is not a happy time. His opportunity to excel in academic life, building on a base way beyond normal for someone his age (he is only twenty when he returns home), is grabbed from him not because he isn't smart enough but because his family can't afford it. Sam sinks into a depression when he is back in his home town.

This is one of many depressions that Sam has and will have throughout his life. The words are different to describe the disease and its effects in the eighteenth century, but Boswell writes later that this bout is a "morbid melancholy" and "horrible hypochondria." The words for the symptoms as Boswell describes them are familiar even today: "perpetual irritation, fretfulness, and impatience; and with a dejection, gloom, and despair, which made existence misery."

And frankly Sam never recovers from the habit of depression. "From this dismal malady he never afterwards was perfectly relieved; and all his labours, and all his enjoyments, were but temporary interruptions of its baleful influence." Sam's misery is understandable. He's back home again, where he doesn't want to be, having had a taste of life among educated and wealthy people. And he hates the work he seems to be destined for.

The first couple of years of the 1730's are bleak ones for Sam. In the midst of an extended period of unemployment, his father becomes sick and ultimately dies in early December 1731.

DIGRESSION
What Sam Looked Like

Sam's physical appearance, and his physical *presence,* often come up in the comments by people who are writing about him later in his life. Sometimes they are simply reporting their perceptions about what he looked like and how he acted, but sometimes—due to the nature of some of his ailments—they are mocking him or pointing out something they find odd or unusual.

He is "unusually tall and strong." Sam is about 1.8 metres (5 foot 11 to 6 feet) tall while other learned men in the city with whom he clubbed are anywhere from 15 to 30 centimetres (6 inches to a full foot) shorter. He is "large, robust, I may say approaching to the gigantick." When she first meets him, Sam's eventual step-daughter Lucy notes that "his appearance was very forbidding" and "his immense structure of bones was hideously striking to the eye." Other words used to describe his body include "giant" and "stout." He is "lean and lank" in his youth (twenty-four years old), but gains weight as he gets older.

The scrofula that Sam was born with also ultimately leaves scars which are "deeply visible." Scrofula is a form of tuberculosis, generally affecting the lymph nodes in the neck. It causes abscesses which burst through the skin and cause running sores, and when those heal, they leave scars.

Beyond his body's dimensions, people also often mention other aspects, sometimes as a means of criticizing him, and sometimes just as reporting what they see. His friend Hester Thrale says that though he was near-sighted, "yet his eyes, though of a light grey colour, were so wild, so piercing, and at times so fierce, that fear was, I believe, the first emotion in the hearts of all his beholders." There are comments about his hair, too, in an era when men generally wore wigs: "he also wore his hair, which was straight and stiff, and separated behind"—Sam is *wearing his hair* in the sense that he *isn't* wearing a wig.

And finally, one of the dominant things that people notice is what are sometimes called his "tics" or "gesticulations" or a whole range of other descriptions. Parts of his body are almost always moving:

- "He often had, seemingly, convulsive starts and odd gesticulations, which tended to excite at once surprize and ridicule"
- He is "always shifting his body when he is seated, and always moving his jaw like an ox chewing the cud"
- "His mouth is almost continually opening and shutting, as if he was chewing. He has a strange method of frequently twirling his fingers, and twisting his hands. His body is in continual agitation, *seesawing* up and down; his feet are never a moment quiet; and, in short, his whole person is in *perpetual motion*"

The inimitable Boswell brings together all the details entailed in Sam just *sitting*:

> While talking or even musing as he sat in his chair, he commonly held his head to one side towards his right shoulder, and shook it in a tremulous manner, moving his body backwards and forwards, and rubbing his left knee in the same direction, with the palm of his hand. In the intervals of articulating he made various sounds with his mouth, sometimes as if ruminating, or what is called chewing the cud, sometimes giving a half whistle, sometimes making his tongue play backwards from the roof of his mouth, as if clucking like a hen, and sometimes protruding it against his upper gums in front, as if pronouncing quickly under his breath, *too, too, too*: all this accompanied sometimes with a thoughtful look, but more frequently with a smile.

Those movements of his body are involuntary. Sam is not putting on a show or trying to be eccentric. Scholars now generally agree that he suffered from Tourette syndrome, which can manifest itself in a wide range of involuntary tics in both speaking (from grunting to swearing) and in movement (eye-rolling, flicking, movement of the arms), and often all in combination.

So Sam makes quite a sight when people first meet him. Combine all of the above with the facts that he also disdained fashion and wasn't always fastidious about personal hygiene. But when they hear him speak, they know that his brain and eloquence and imagination are exceptional.

CHAPTER 2

MARRIED MAN AND TEACHER, 1732–1737

SAM IS TWENTY-THREE YEARS OLD in late 1732 when his good friend Edmund Hector, whom he's known since childhood, invites him to come visit him at his place in Birmingham, a large industrial city about 30 km south of Lichfield. Sam and Hector get along well, and Sam is a social, outgoing sort who meets a few other people as well during his time in the city.

One of them is a man named Thomas Warren, a bookseller—what we would call a *publisher* today—in whose house Hector is a lodger. Warren is starting a new weekly newspaper called the *Birmingham Journal* and he asks Sam to contribute. The offer comes at a good time for him and provides Sam with an activity to counter his ongoing depression. He writes one and then several other pieces for Warren. But there is some bad news which frustrates those of us today who would like to see what kinds of things Sam was writing at such a young age. Unfortunately, no issues of the *Journal* survive today from the time when Sam was in Birmingham—and in fact the one single original issue, also without any of

Sam's writing, that did survive until the mid-twentieth century (number 28 for May 21, 1733) is now lost as well, and only a copy of it survives.

Hector eventually decides to move out of Warren's house and by June 1733 Sam himself is also living elsewhere, in a room in the house of F. Jervis. The freedom and the time he has on his hands also inspire him to take on another writing project while he is still in Birmingham. He mentions to Hector that while he was at Oxford he read a French translation of the memoir of a Portuguese Jesuit, a man named Jerónimo Lobo, and his experiences in Abyssinia (what we now call Ethiopia) in the early seventeenth century. Sam thinks that it would be a good idea to translate the French version into English but also to make it shorter: it "might be an useful and profitable publication."

Both Hector and Warren encourage him and Sam starts in on it but—a lifetime habit—he is slow and procrastinates, because he doesn't have a hard deadline. Hector tries to prod and encourage him by saying that the poor printer and his family are suffering because the printer can't take on another job until the translation is finished. This finally gets Sam moving: "He lay in bed with the book, which was a quarto, before him, and dictated while Hector wrote. Mr. Hector carried the sheets to the press, and corrected almost all the proof sheets, very few of which were even seen by Johnson." His persistence pays off and the book is finished. It is ultimately published in 1735 as *A Voyage to Abyssinia* and is Sam's very first major work in prose. He is paid 5 guineas (about £800 today).

Apart from Warren and Hector, another important person whom Sam meets for the first time while in Birmingham is Elizabeth Porter, wife of Harry Porter. Harry dies on September 3 at the age of forty-three, leaving behind Elizabeth and their three children, including a daughter named Lucy. Though Sam is only a young man of twenty-five by now, and Elizabeth—whom he calls "Tetty"—a forty-six-year-old widow, they are attracted to each other. Not that of course beauty is the main thing that drives love, but whatever it is they see in each other physically is not shared or appreciated by friends and family, especially those who are opposed to the match. Tetty's daughter Lucy finds Sam "forbidding" and goes on to detail some aspects of his looks that she also finds offensive. (See the "Digression: What Sam Looked Like.") These are ones that people will notice all through Sam's life: tall and "immense"; scarred with scrofula; wigless; "convulsive" tics.

As for the attraction, physical or otherwise, it is not one-sided. Tetty describes Sam as "the most sensible man that I ever saw in my life." That's saying something, as she is a woman who has had experience and met a lot of people. Tetty demonstrates her character and discernment here. She can see past the physical imperfections and view the important essence of the man, even when others around her are complaining about how ridiculous it is for her even to consider such a mate. She is consistent later in her life with him as well, when generally she is a strong supporter of whatever Sam does. She can't be dismissed as simply a middle-aged woman with few other prospects who is just grasping at the first man who shows her any attention.

Alas, Boswell describes in his florid style how Sam has behaved himself sexually up till now, but now that Elizabeth Porter is available, his thoughts become focused: "In a man whom religious education has secured from licentious indulgences, the passion of love, when once it has seized him, is exceedingly strong; being unimpaired by dissipation, and totally concentrated in one object. This was experienced by Johnson, when he became the fervent admirer of Mrs. Porter, after her first husband's death."

There's a lot to unpack there stylistically, but essentially he is saying that religion kept Sam from having casual sex, but when he fell in love his sexual attraction was strong when it was focused on just one woman. This is of course unfair and ungenerous to Sam, as well as a pretty simplistic analysis of the situation. Just because a man has gone a long time without sex doesn't necessarily mean that there's a build-up of desire that causes him to become too attached and attentive to the first woman who shows him any interest. Boswell famously kept a journal of his escapades in London with prostitutes and other women when he was in his early twenties, and so he may be projecting his own tendencies onto Sam.

Tetty is described by some people just as ungenerously and harshly as Sam himself is. David Garrick, one of Sam's former students, calls her "very fat, with a bosom of more than ordinary protuberance" and "swelled cheeks of a florid red, produced by thick painting, and increased by the liberal use of cordials." What is it with people and the physical appearance of others? Sam has made a connection with her and they both have their reasons for liking each other. Passion can happen powerfully between two people, regardless of the scars on one person's neck and the other person's overuse of makeup.

He has therefore had a pretty successful trip to Birmingham, publishing his first book and falling in love, so that by the time he returns to Lichfield in February 1735 he's a more confident young man. Focusing on the literary side of things, biographer Peter Martin says that "the main effect of Birmingham was that now he wanted to earn money by writing. He was more certain than ever that he did not want to sell books. He wanted to produce them." Back home, Sam starts writing in his diary (*Annals*) again, including a list of various classic works in Greek and Latin which he plans to read.

On the romantic side of things, there is momentum as well, and in fact just five months later, on July 9, 1735, Tetty and Sam get married in the town of Derby, about 70 km northeast of Birmingham, in St Werburgh's Church. (The two buildings of the church still stand and over the years it has been closed and then opened again for services. For a while it was a market and Chinese restaurant, but since 2017 it has been offering church services again.) Some scholars suggest that the ceremony was not held in either of their home towns because both families disapproved of the marriage. As mentioned, Tetty is forty-six and Sam is twenty-five. The average age at the time for a man to get married is twenty-nine. As for Tetty, widows like other people rendered single do remarry in the eighteenth century. "Remarriage remained common," one historian writes, with about eight percent of the women getting married being previously widowed, and about fifteen percent of all weddings including at least one member of the new couple who is *remarrying*. Remarriage is certainly not a stigma or something unusual.

Part of the reason is how different life was then compared to the present. Life is more uniform and scheduled now, but in the eighteenth century, "because what kind of work you do and when you went to work varies enormously in age, then people's movements that map life course action are quite different." People married early or remarried because many died young, too. Even the situation of a young man marrying an older woman was not uncommon, "because lots of journeymen marry their master's wives when the master dies," and it was not unusual either for the members of the couple to live in different cities as Tetty and Sam do.

Sam goes back to Birmingham so that they can travel together from there to the wedding ceremony in Derby.

The transportation is not luxurious—by horseback—and frankly Sam makes it worse by being impatient. He's a young man, this is his first love, and he apparently doesn't know the manners and customs of treating such a person nicely. He is either displaying a macho determination not to be dominated, or inexperience with the practical generosity of love:

> At first she told me that I rode too fast, and she could not keep up with me; and, when I rode a little slower, she passed me, and complained that I lagged behind. I was not to be made the slave of caprice; and I resolved to begin as I meant to end. I therefore pushed on briskly, till I was fairly out of her sight. The road lay between two hedges, so I was sure she could not miss it; and I contrived that she should soon come up [catch up] with me. When she did, I observed her to be in tears.

Eventually, the nuptials over, they make it back to Lichfield, a newly married couple. One of the first things they set their minds to is a career for Sam, or even just a job for now. He wants to be a teacher, and even though he certainly has the knowledge for it, he lacks a university degree. However, there also turn out to be other reasons why Sam would be, as we might say today, a *difficult hire*. Five weeks after the wedding, Sam's lawyer friend Gilbert Walmesley writes a letter to Henry Greswold in support of Sam's candidacy for the headmaster position at the school in the town of Solihull, about 40 km south of Lichfield.

The reply that comes back from Greswold a couple of weeks later (August 30) is a rejection. Sam isn't even interviewed—they simply have taken "some time to make enquiry of the caracter of Mr. Johnson." Those are fancy words for *we asked a few people what he was like.* They conclude that though he's an excellent scholar and that the job at Solihull might even be a bit beneath him, he has some personal and physical faults which make them say no. In short, they are worried that he might scare the young boy students: "he has such a way of distorting his Face" that they "think it may affect some young ladds," a reference to the manifestations of his Tourette's.

So with jobs scarce and Sam's appearance and lack of degree credentials likely to be a hindrance, they move to plan B. Tetty has come to the marriage with money, as much as £800 (£120,000 today), from the death of her former husband. They rent a farmhouse in Edial which they intend not only to outfit as a school, but also to use as the place where they live and the students will board. They attract only three students, which is better than none, but not sustainable if they are going to make a go at this as their main source of income.

The school operates for several months, but Sam still has, at best, only a few more students in addition to the original three. He advertises in the *Gentleman's Magazine* in the June and July 1736 issues: "At Edial, near *Litchfield* in *Staffordshire,* Young Gentlemen are

Boarded, and Taught the *Latin* and *Greek* Languages, by Samuel Johnson."

Sam is prepared for any additional students the ads might attract. In spite of his general disorganization about things and details, just as in later life with other endeavours, he always has a plan and he somehow manages to get the job done, though often later than he has promised. For the school, he draws up a "plan of education" with details about all the classical authors he wants to teach them about. But as one scholar points out, his main principle makes the connection between why it is important to study ancient authors in the first place: "The greatest and most necessary task still remains, to attain a habit of expression, without which knowledge is of little use. This is necessary in Latin, and more necessary in English; and can only be acquired by a daily imitation of the best and correctest authors." It all comes down to writing and self-expression. It is no good knowing about the writings of others, if you are not able to write about those others—or anything else—yourself.

During this time, Sam's unemployment and especially the differences in their characters have put some strain on his marriage. In these early years, though, their differences shouldn't be exaggerated. They are still newlyweds and still getting used to the idea of living with each other. Like any married couple, Tetty and Sam experience both bliss and bickering.

For example, she likes a clean house more than he does. "My wife had a particular reverence for cleanliness, and desired the praise of neatness in her dress and furniture, as many ladies do ... 'A clean floor is so comfortable,' she would say sometimes, by way of twitting [criticizing]; till at last I told her that I thought we had had talk enough about the *floor*, we would now have a touch at the *ceiling*."

Other times, Tetty is ready with a quick response. Sam complains many times about the quality of his dinner— so often that one time she says to him when he is in the middle of saying grace: "Nay, hold, Mr. Johnson, and do not make a farce of thanking God for a dinner which in a few minutes you will protest not eatable."

Sam's behaviour is hard to justify, but he is not cavalier about the arguments they have. He doesn't accept them as simply a negative aspect of a marriage that has no enduring effects: "all quarrels ought to be avoided studiously, particularly conjugal ones, as no one can possibly tell where they may end; besides that lasting dislike is often the consequence of occasional disgust, and that the cup of life is surely bitter enough, without squeezing in the hateful rind of resentment."

In spite of the curriculum and the advertising for the school, it is not a success. It lasts another few months but Sam eventually accepts the reality and closes it later in the year. It marks the failure of yet another attempt to become a teacher, not to mention the loss of Tetty's money in setting up the school, and so the still new couple have to recalibrate.

While he's been trying to teach, Sam has also been corresponding with a potential employer in another field: writing. The man is Edward Cave, publisher of the *Gentleman's Magazine*, a new venture he started in 1731. In fact, this is not only *Cave's* first magazine, but what some describe as the first magazine ever published. Its distinction is being the first periodical which covers a wide variety of news and general information, rather than being a scientific periodical on a very specific topic. Cave's use of the word *magazine* in the title is the first time that it has ever been used in English in that sense.

In 1734 Sam is still a young man of twenty-five. He sees an opportunity to rescue himself, and he has the confidence to act. He writes a letter to Cave from Birmingham, half confidently, half naively, basically saying that he has the skills to make the magazine better. This is the opening sentence (note that the word *defect* at the time could simply mean lacking something, and not really be calling attention to a fault): "As you appear no less sensible than Your Readers of the defects of your Poetical Article, You will not be displeased, if, in order to the improvement of it, I communicate to You the sentiments of a person, who will undertake on reasonable terms sometimes to fill a column."

Sam goes on to give some details of what he could supply to the magazine, including original poems, critical commentary on "ancient or modern" authors, the reprinting of "forgotten poems that deserve revival," and other "loose pieces." He signs himself as Cave's "humble servant" and gives him instructions on where to reply.

There's a great combination here of confidence and insecurity, typical of a young man who realizes that he has intelligence and talent, but who has been beaten down by recent events. The confidence is in his having the courage to send this letter at all, and the latter (perhaps) in choosing to hide himself behind the false name of "S. Smith." Cave does respond to the letter a week later, and though we don't know what he said, the end result is that Sam is not hired. At least not this time.

DIGRESSION
Life in London in the Eighteenth Century

The following is not meant to be a comprehensive overview of social and business life in England during the century. Just the opposite. It's a short guide to major facts, events, and practices, in order to give you an idea of some of the milieu that Sam lived in.

Population

The population of England as of the latest (2021) census is 56.5 million and the population of London is 8.6 million. Figures vary in different sources for the same statistics in the eighteenth century, but one estimates that in the middle of the century the populations were 6 million and 650,000, respectively. London was far more populous than any other place in the country: even by the end of the century, all other cities had populations of less than 100,000.

Money

The currency, then as now, was the British pound, but its value in the eighteenth century was very different from what it is in the early twenty-first century. Sources vary wildly on what the conversion factor should be. By what number should you multiply an amount of money that you read about in the eighteenth century, in order to have at least a reasonable estimate of how much that is in today's pounds?

One of Sam's scholarly biographers recommends 100 as the conversion factor, that is, if something costs £5 then it would cost £500 today; another scholar recommends a conversion factor of 250. The Official Data Foundation's inflation calculator compares the pound in 1750 to the pound in 2021 and comes up with a conversion factor of about 225. A company called Statista provides information on the value of the pound from the year 1209 to 2019. Its charts show a decrease in the pound over the course of the century, with the conversion being about 207 in 1700 and 115 in 1799. And the British National Archives has a currency converter covering the value of the pound from the year 1270 but only going up to 2017. It gives about 105 for the year 1700, but with the value declining in the latter half of the century, reaching only about 75 in 1790.

So, what's a reader to conclude? Throughout this book, I have somewhat unscientifically assigned a value of £150 for the eighteenth-century pound in today's terms, and have indicated the resulting modern value after any amount mentioned.

Finally, another way to get a sense of relative value is to look at things more broadly, and with examples:

> For much of the 18th century a regular income—hardly ever attainable, I should add—of 75p a week (say £40 a year) would provide security and reasonable comfort for a family of man, woman and two children; a pound a week

would be considered good money for anyone working with their hands, even a junior clerk; and a gentleman could manage to keep up a decent appearance on £ 200 a year.

One further note. You also see other currency terms used in eighteenth-century writing. Some of the other pieces of currency at the time, in descending order of value, were:

- the guinea (1 = £1.05)
- the pound (£1)
- the crown (4 = £1)
- the shilling (20 = £1)
- the pence (100 = £1)

Clothing

There were no stores where you bought clothing off the rack in eighteenth-century England. Everything was tailor-made. The tailor would actually come to the homes of wealthy people, who would choose their fabrics and materials for the tailor to make the dress or suit or other clothing item from. The wealthy were also very fashion conscious, and so when fashion changed, or when an article of clothing became worn out, or when they just got tired of wearing it, they would tend to simply give it to their servants.

The servants would then either alter the item to fit them—most were very skilled at this—or would simply sell it if it didn't suit them. There was a huge market for second-hand clothing. Again, the poorer people would buy what they liked and then alter it to fit them. Their children wore clothing that was originally fitted for adults, but these too would be bought second-hand and cut and altered extensively to fit them.

Neither men nor women wore underwear. Men would tuck the long tails of their shirts between their legs and wear their britches over that. Women wore a *shift*, that is, a long night dress (usually white) and then wore their outside clothing over that. They wore nothing like panties or any other kind of modern-day underwear.

Men wore wigs as a part of their everyday dress, not just for fancy occasions. Even teenage boys wore them, and even boys as young as five years old.

Personal Hygiene

So, how clean were people underneath those clothes? One scholar writes that "it's a myth that people liked to go dirty." Sometimes poor people were dirty due to necessity and not by choice. As for clothing and linen and the like, the poor had less of these anyway and so they had to spend less time and money cleaning it all. The wealthy washed more often and late in the century even had "plunge baths" in their gardens—cold water, but they could conveniently wash themselves. Keeping their clothes and linens clean required a lot of time for the wealthy, and so they generally employed washing women to come in every month or two to clean what by then would be a huge pile of clothes and linen. The washing women would spend a couple of days washing everything and hanging it out to dry, and would return in another month or two when everything was dirty again.

Publishing

There was a huge increase in the number and the types of books published during the eighteenth century. One scholar calls the century "transformational," with a revolution in readership:

> A gentle increase in literacy led to more people buying books, periodicals and newspapers— and a much enlarged second-hand market and more borrowing from newly established libraries. But even more significantly, the proportion of the population that was already buying books was now able to buy more... In the second half of the eighteenth century, for example, there was an extraordinary demand for magazines and publications aimed specifically at women or children.

But at the same time, the technology for publishing them had not changed much since the very first books had been printed in England in the late fifteenth century, using moveable metal type and a wooden printing press.

The typical way that a writer published a book was through "subscription." They would publish a "proposal" for a book they intended to write, and those who were interested in reserving their copy of the book would pay the publisher or writer in advance. Sometimes the book was just about to be published, and sometimes it might be months or years away. The proposal could be just a short advertisement in a periodical, or (in the case of Sam's dictionary, for example) a fairly substantial publication in itself.

"Patronage" was a common practice. A patron was a wealthy person or a member of the peerage who agreed to partially fund the book and to have their name associated with it, generally in exchange for receiving very praiseful acknowledgement when the book was eventually published. The basic advantage to the patron was the little bit of added publicity and fame, and to the author was the encouragement of sales of their book that could come from being in effect endorsed by a noble.

But depending on the specific arrangement between the author and the patron, there could be more benefits for each of them. A patron could even find them an employment position, as well as what we could call today "significant networking and marketing opportunities for the author which came from having a known name attached to a text." For the patron, one scholar says that "patrons saw dedications as a powerful tool for creating a public identity for themselves that not only affected their reputation but also ... influenced the way in which the public received and reacted to such texts ... Patrons organised their correspondence with their clients into ... letter-books and miscellanies in order to influence public perception of themselves and frame themselves as arbiters of taste." The heyday of patronage was the first half of the century, but by the second half it was waning.

The first copyright act (often called the "Statute of Anne") wasn't passed in England until 1710. It gave authors copyright of their publications—previously it was the publishers and printers who held the right exclusively—but the right was not given to authors in perpetuity, was not a "personal right." They were given copyright for fourteen years, renewable for another fourteen years, but then the book became part of what is still called the "public domain." This meant that anyone and everyone then had a right to the publication and could print it as they saw fit. But even when the law was technically in effect, there was a lot of pirating of published books during much of the eighteenth century.

Time Change

In our own century, *time change* refers to those dates in the spring and fall where, in most countries and in most smaller jurisdictions in those countries, the time jumps ahead one hour in the spring and falls back an hour in the fall. And I suppose another type of time change happens in leap years, when we add a day onto the end of February.

There was a more major time change that took place in the eighteenth century in England, which is useful to note because you may see some remnants of it in older texts, or digitized versions of them, that you happen to read. There is a long and fascinating history of the reasons for the change, but in simple practical terms what happened in England was that the Julian calendar was replaced by the Gregorian calendar (the one we still use today) in 1752, and to rectify the discrepancy between the two, the Calendar (New Style) Act 1750 decreed that eleven days would be *eliminated* from the calendar in 1752: September 2 was followed immediately by September 14. Nothing happened in England from September 3 to September 13, because those days did not occur!

The dates in books and letters are often qualified with the abbreviations *O.S.* or *N.S.* (for *Old Style* and *New Style*) as people adapted to the change. In Sam's case specifically, when he was born in 1709 the Julian calendar was still being used, so you sometimes read him referring to his birthday as being on September 7.

CHAPTER 3

WRITING FOR MONEY, 1737–1749

SAM IS FAMOUSLY ASSOCIATED WITH three main places in England: Lichfield, where he was born; Oxford, where he spent about a year at university; and London, where he made his name, his money, and spent most of his life. Of course, he sometimes visited the other two places, and others in England, but when you think of Sam you think of London. And his feeling for the city is summed up in one of the most famous of his sayings: "Sir, when a man is tired of London, he is tired of life; for there is in London all that life can afford."

It isn't until 1737, when he is twenty-seven years old, that Sam heads out for London for the first time in his life. He is a married man by now, though his wife isn't coming with him yet (she will join him later in the year). Instead, on March 2, he and his friend and former student David Garrick set out by horse for London. They have only the one horse, and so they "rode and tied" in order to get to their destination, "each taking turns to ride ahead, tie up the horse to a wayside post and walk on." This is a common practice at the time in cases where you have two travellers but only one horse. Each person has to walk a while and each person, and the horse, gets a break.

It is a journey of hope. Sam has some pretty major failures and disappointments behind him in the two other towns: the necessity of dropping out of university after he ran out of money in Oxford, and the failed attempts at setting up as a teacher near Lichfield. He does have some successes and potential too though. He has published a book and he has with him the draft of a play called *Irene* which he started writing in 1735. It takes them less than a week to travel the approximately 210 km to the big city. Both of the travellers also suffer family losses on the way: Johnson's brother Nathaniel dies (at the age of 25), and Garrick's father also dies.

Sam famously said later in life that "No man but a blockhead ever wrote, except for money," and when he arrives in London he applies this practical (if a bit overstated) attitude. On July 12 he writes to Edward Cave again, the publisher of the *Gentleman's Magazine*. This time he has a very specific proposal: a translation of the *History of the Council of Trent*, originally published in 1619 by the Italian priest Paolo Sarpi. (The Council of Trent was an ecumenical council of the Catholic Church, held between 1545 and 1563, in response to the Protestant Reformation.)

Sam writes very confidently to Cave with a ready answer to whether another English translation should be written when one has already been published: "If it be answered that the History is already in English, it must be remembered that... You cannot read three Pages of [it], without discovering that the Stile is capable of great Improvements." In other words: mine would be better written. And if Cave doesn't think the improvement of style will be enough, Johnson has a further reason why his translation would be useful: "It took them less than a week, we may hope that the Addition of the Notes will turn the Ballance in our Favour, considering the Reputation of the Annotator." Again, that's pretty explicit confidence from a young man with no substantial writing credentials to back up his claims of being a superior annotator.

Cave does not accept this original proposal, but does take it on the following year. Boswell provides the details of an agreement between Sam and Cave whereby between August 2, 1738, and April 21, 1739, Sam is paid over £49 (about £7,500 today) for the translation. Later in August though, Sam hasn't made much progress on the translation, and so he writes to Cave again: "I [...] have met with impediments which I hope, are now at an end, and if you find the Progress hereafter not such as You have a right to expect, You can easily stimulate [prod] a negligent Translator."

This is typical delay and procrastination on Sam's part—he starts young and it is a habit that continues much of his life—and of course in many cases in which it is understandable because the project is large and he has underestimated the time to complete it, he is often very self-critical at what he perceives as his own laziness. In this case, Sam's plea to Cave and his follow-through are ultimately unsuccessful, but not because of Sam's slackness. It turns out that *another* Johnson—first name, John, a librarian—is also working on the same translation, and as Boswell puts it: "Several light skirmishes passed between the rival translators, in the newspapers of the day; and the consequence was, that they destroyed each other, for neither of them went on with the work." And so in the end the book is doomed. The combination of Sam being behind in the writing, the confusion and rivalry over two books on the same topic at the same time by two Johnsons—and most importantly, the ultimate reluctance of the publisher, Cave, to keep funding a book that he is worried would not sell—all that leads to the ceasing of any further work on it by both author and publisher.

Sam's experience as a staff writer and editor for the *Gentleman's Magazine* is one of the few times when he mostly just cranks out copy for money. This is early in his career, from 1738 to 1745, when he is in his late twenties to mid-thirties. Cave has turned it into an enormous journalistic and (for him at least) financial success.

The title page of the first issue from January 1731 gives a good idea of the range of miscellaneous contents and formats the magazine contained:

A view of the Weekly *Essays* and *Controversies*... Poetry... *Domestick* Occurrences, *viz.* Births, Deaths, Marriages, Preferments,

> Casualties, Burials and Christenings in *Lon-don*... Melancholy Effects of Credulity in *Witch-craft*... Prices of Goods and Stocks, and a List of Bankrupts... A correct List of the Sheriffs for the current Year... Remarkable *Advertise-ments*... *Foreign* Affairs, with an Introduction to this Year's History... Books and pamphlets publish'd... Observations in *Gardening*, and the Fairs in *Feb*.

This period is a productive, creative, and successful time for Sam, and he starts to see the first hints that a literary career might be a possibility for him. In October 1737 he finally finishes the only play he ever writes—*Irene*, the one he had in draft form with him when he first moved to London—but what he doesn't know is that it will be about *twelve years* before the play is finally produced for the stage.

The year 1738 is a special one: his first piece to be published in his new home of London appears in the *Gentleman's Magazine* in March. It's a poem titled "Ad Urbanum," written entirely in Latin, but (significantly) signed "S. J." The poem is addressed to Cave, and the *Urban-* refers to Cave's own pseudonym for himself (Sylvanus Urban, meaning "a country and city man"). It is part of a full page worth of praise for Cave by various writers, countering rival and jealous publishers *"whose Names are not worth the mention"* for their criticisms of him. It probably helps Sam get his full-time job at the magazine.

Sam carries out a real variety of work. He writes biographies. He does translations. He edits the contributions of other writers. He even contributes some of his own poems. One of his greatest contributions is as what may be called a parliamentary reporter. It is illegal at the time to write directly about the speeches in the House of Commons, and so Cave's method of getting around that restriction is instead to publish "Debates in the Senate of Magna Lilliputia," with a nod to the kingdom of Lilliput in Jonathan Swift's *Gulliver's Travels*, where the inhabitants are one-twelfth the size of regular humans (but equal in ridiculability). The names of the real parliamentarians are barely disguised in the reports from the fictional Lilliputia (for example, Prime Minister Sir Robert Walpole is Sir Rub. Walelop or Sir Retrob Walelop). At first, Sam's job is to simply edit the debates as written by the current editor, William Guthrie, but soon Sam's skill is recognized, and in the summer of 1741 Cave makes him the sole editor of the debates. He retains this assignment until early 1744. Sam is actually one of several well-known writers in the eighteenth and nineteenth centuries who have been parliamentary reporters (notable others are Samuel Taylor Coleridge, William Hazlitt, and Charles Dickens). Sam's focus is satire and "creativity," whereas the others tended toward simple "accuracy."

The successes continue. A poem which is today recognized as one of Sam's best is published in May. Cave generously arranges for "London" to be published not in the *Gentleman's Magazine* but separately by the publisher Robert Dodsley. Sam is paid 10 guineas (about £1,600 today) for the copyright. And then near the end of the year, Sam finally gets to publish something about Sarpi—still not the *Council of Trent*, but a biography of Sarpi himself. It is published in the November issue of the magazine, and unlike the anonymously published "London" poem, there are at least Sam's initials, "S. J.," at the end, and "S. Johnson" in the full title. The biography is short, taking up only about three pages in the magazine. Still, it's a good sign. Sam is being assigned not only the anonymous work of the "Debates," but is getting close to having an explicit byline.

Sam and Tetty have a series of different living relationships during this period: she still living in Lichfield and he in London, both living in Lichfield or London together, and sometimes each living apart even though both of them are in London. In the summer of 1737 Sam moves back to Lichfield to be with her, and stays until October to finally finish writing *Irene*. That done, the couple moves to London, ultimately ending up at 6 Castle Street. They live together for a while, but eventually Sam moves out and Tetty ends up remaining there until January 1740. This is an early sign of the troubled marriage they have ahead of them, when they will spend both short and long periods physically separated, among other problems.

It may be just a coincidence that Sam and Tetty live apart during the whole time that he has a friendship with Richard Savage, an infamous poet in the city who also contributes to the magazine. Their friendship is messy and intense, but Sam, now and throughout his life, demonstrates a high tolerance for things and people that do not run smoothly. As one biographer points out, they meet in 1738 when Sam is an "unknown" writer who has been in London for about a year, and Savage is well known and "notorious." He is a regular drinker and often borrows money from friends who eventually get used to the idea that they will never be repaid.

It says something about the life he led that his involvement in a five-way fight outside a coffeehouse in which one of the servers is injured and a bystander is actually killed by Savage or one of his two friends—that *this* is not the defining incident in his life. One of the friends is convicted of only manslaughter, but Savage and the other friend are convicted of murder and sentenced to death. Several people write and otherwise plea on his behalf to spare his life, but it is ultimately a countess's appeal to the queen that gets him pardoned. This all happened when he was about thirty years old, about ten years before Sam meets him.

Savage's obsession throughout his life is his campaign to prove that he is the illegitimate son of Anne Gerard (née Mason). She was only fifteen in 1683 when she married Charles Gerard, and the separation and divorce proceedings lasted longer than the marriage. While waiting for the divorce to be finalized she conceived two children (Anne and Richard) with another man, the fourth Earl Rivers, but claimed they both died at birth.

Modern historians are divided about her claim. She inherited the title Lady Macclesfield when the divorce was finalized in 1698, and remarried two years later, her ex-husband dying the following year.

The friendship between Sam and Savage is an "invisible" one. Typically they wander the streets of London late into the night and early morning: "Those who know nothing else of his early life can envision in Hogarthian detail Johnson in his ill-fitting great-coat and Savage dressed like a decayed dandy, wandering the street for want of a lodging and inveighing against fortune and the Prime Minister." Savage is usually broke, borrows money from friends that he doesn't pay back, and squanders what he does have on alcohol and other vices. And then he asks his dwindling number of friends for more money.

After a frustrating and dissipated life, during which he tests the patience of many friends, Savage dies on August 1, 1743. Sam is fast to write a full biography of the man, which is published about six months later by Cave. Sam always expressed thanks to Cave for his assistance, but in 1745 Sam has bigger projects in mind, and he finally gives up the editing work for the *Gentleman's Magazine*.

One of the projects is cataloguing the library of Robert Harley, second Earl of Oxford, who died in June 1741. His enormous collection of books is bought by the bookseller Thomas Osborne, who intends to sell the titles separately and so turn a profit, but the size of it makes the prospect daunting. Osborne asks Sam, who is particularly in need of money at this time of his life, to do the job, but they both underestimate the amount of work necessary to catalogue fifty thousand volumes. Still, Sam gets started with a very organized plan in mind: "the books shall be distributed into their distinct classes, and every class ranged with some regard to the age of the writers; that every book shall be accurately described; that the peculiarities of editions shall be re-marked, and observations from the authors of literary history occasionally interspersed." Two volumes are published in 1743 and another two in 1744, but that is the last of Sam's work on the catalogue, as he had nothing to do with the fifth and final volume in 1745.

Sam has some tastes of literary success as well before the decade is over. His poem "The Vanity of Human Wishes" is published in January 1749 by Robert Dodsley. This remains one of his best and best-known poems. It's written in imitation of the tenth satire in the collection of sixteen written by the classical Roman poet Juvenal. Satire is not an often-used genre by Sam (in contrast to his partial contemporary Jonathan Swift, who of course revelled in it). Sam's poem is a litany of the bad things that befall our species, many of them brought on by human vices. These lines are typical of the attitude of there being no escape from some sort of harm in one's life:

> Deign on the passing world to turn thine eyes,
> And pause awhile from letters, to be wise;

> There mark what ills the scholar's life assail,
> Toil, envy, want, the patron, and the jail.
> See nations slowly wise, and meanly just,
> To buried merit raise the tardy bust.

His other success is his play, *Irene*, the one he brought unfinished with him when he left Lichfield for London twelve years earlier. It is finally produced and opens February 6, 1749, running for nine nights. The producer is David Garrick, who has become by now a famous actor and theatre owner in London. *Irene* is staged at Garrick's Drury Lane Theatre, and both Sam himself and critics then and since acknowledge that it is mediocre at best. The story is set in the fifteenth century, and Irene, a Christian, is captured by sultan Mohamet (based on the Ottoman Mehmed the Conqueror, who conquered the Byzantine Empire). He convinces her to become his Muslim queen and the play ends tragically when Irene is caught up in the palace politics and ultimately killed. When Mahomet is told that she was not plotting against him, he is heartbroken:

> O seize me, Madness!—Did she call on me!
> I feel, I see the ruffian's barb'rous rage.
> He seiz'd her melting in the fond appeal,
> And stopp'd the heav'nly voice that call'd on me.

Irene was a financial success for him. He earned about £200 (£30,000 today) for the performances and another £100 (£15,000) when he sold the script to Dodsley.

DIGRESSION
Sam's Depression and Harshness with Himself

Sam's literary legacy is different from the legacy of a lot of other writers because many people know about his *life*, thanks to Boswell's famous biography, but they may have read little or none of Sam's actual writing. They know about the anecdotes that Boswell meticulously collected, as well as the quips and sayings from his conversation, but his books and essays are often forgotten. Perhaps the one exception is that people know that he compiled a dictionary of English and so they may remember the definitions of some of the words. The disadvantage is that modern readers are missing out on some of the best prose ever written in English, but one advantage is that they know about Sam the person, some of his characteristics, some of his virtues, and some of his faults. Not all of these are found in Boswell though. Some are found only in his published writing, but especially also in Sam's personal writing—journals, prayers, letters, sermons, and so on.

Many people know him as a very *human* person. They can sometimes identify with aspects of his life and character. One scholar says that Sam "agonized about his religious belief and ... it's that human side of him that attracts me to him ... that independence of thought and very human vulnerability, proneness to depression, self-doubt, and so on." These are frankly some of the things that have drawn me to Sam all these years too. He led by any standard a highly productive life, but one that he was often unsatisfied with, one that made him extremely self-critical for not doing more, one that made him suffer recurring bouts of depression. Sam defined *melancholy* in his own dictionary as "a gloomy, pensive, discontented temper," and he was afflicted with it all through his life. Scholars generally consider it a disposition that he inherited from his father, and whether or not the origin is that simple, it's certainly true that Sam was repeatedly depressed, especially during times of hardship (what we might call *stress* today) or failure, or after not achieving a goal. Boswell wrote about it in his biography, describing Sam's father in terms that could easily be applied to Sam himself: "Mr. Michael Johnson was a man of a large and robust body, and of a strong and active mind; yet... there was in him... a general sensation of gloomy wretchedness."

There were many such incidents in Sam's life, but I'll mention just a couple of them. We've already seen one after he was forced to cut short his time at university when the money ran out, and there are others as his life story continues. During one of them, when he was in his mid-fifties, he didn't want to see anyone, but his former tutor from Oxford was allowed in. Sam was "in a deplorable state, sighing, groaning, talking to himself, and restlessly walking from room to room... At one point Johnson cried out, 'I would consent to have a limb amputated to recover my spirits.'"

One of the things that caused him as much distress as comfort was religion and his relationship with the God that he believed in till his death, both when he was good and when he judged himself to be bad. "His faith brought him for the best part of his life little peace," as one scholar puts it. Sam felt that he was repeatedly not living up to the standards set forth in the Bible, and so he would constantly chastise himself for his past actions, and vow to himself and to God that he would do better in the future. He demonstrated not heroism but rather "fragility" when he made these resolutions, very different from the tough and articulate debater who held forth at the clubs and coffee houses.

Self-criticism, setting a very high standard and then being harsh on himself for not meeting it, is a constant theme in Sam's life. On Easter 1753, for example, he composed "a prayer ... against unchastity, idleness, & neglect of publick worship," and he is still haranguing himself about it twenty-three years later in 1776 (Easter again):

> My reigning sin, to which perhaps many others are appendent, is waste of time, and general sluggishness, to which I was always inclined and in part of my life have been almost compelled by morbid melancholy and disturbance of mind. Melancholy has had in me its paroxisms and remissions, but I have not improved the intervals, nor sufficiently resisted my natural inclination,

or sickly habits. I will resolve henceforth to rise at eight in the morning, so far as resolution is proper, and will pray that God will strengthen me. I have begun this morning.

It is easy to sympathize with him generally but also because of his belief that getting up earlier and praying might have much effect on his depressive and anxious mind. He was not naive though. The common thread was that he was resolving the same things repeatedly while at the same time realizing he was human and would need God's help:

When I look back upon resoluti[ons] of improvement and amendments, which have year after year been made and broken, either by negligence, forgetfulness, vicious idleness, casual interruption, or morbid infirmity, when I find that so much of my life has stolen unprofitably away, and that I can descry [observe] by retrospection scarcely a few single days properly and vigorously employed, why do I yet try to resolve again? I try because Reformation is necessary and despair is criminal. I try in humble hope of the help of God.

Perhaps the surprise is that at no point did he ever wonder why God was apparently not helping him with his goals. There was no, "My God, my God, why have you forsaken me?" But this regular ritual of declaring defeat and vowing to do better was not psychologically healthy. The other thing, of course, is that no matter how lazy he was or thought he was, or no matter how late he got up in the morning (or, frankly, in the afternoon), he actually managed to get an extraordinary amount of work done. He worked on three huge writing projects during various stages of his life (the dictionary in his thirties and forties, the edition of Shakespeare's plays in his fifties, and the biographies of poets in his seventies). He wrote two series of essays in his early (the *Rambler*) and late (the *Idler*) forties, and wrote and advised for another one in his mid-forties (*The Adventurer*). He published poetry, a play, a novella, more biography, and political pamphlets. He produced a large quantity of high-quality work over a period of less than fifty years.

CHAPTER 4

THE DICTIONARY, 1746–1755

ONE OF THE GREAT UNDERTAKINGS for which Sam is well known is that he produced a dictionary of the English language. Some people often refer to him as "Dr. Johnson" because of his honorary degree. He was awarded three of them during his lifetime: a master's from Oxford University in 1755; a doctorate from Trinity College Dublin in 1765; and another doctorate, again from Oxford, in 1775. But he never graduated with any degree. But you also sometimes hear him called "Dictionary Johnson" as well—a tribute to how important this book is to his reputation as a writer, but also to how innovative this dictionary was compared to some other English dictionaries which came before it. One scholar even titled the book he wrote about this period of Johnson's life as *Dictionary Johnson*. It's an ironic fact that a man who is now often referred to as "Dr. Johnson" never actually graduated from university.

Sam signs a contract on June 18, 1746, to complete the dictionary in three years. He is paid the large sum of 1,500 guineas (about £240,000 today), enough so that he and his wife Tetty are able to move into a new home around this time. It turns out to be big enough for the large space necessary to get the dictionary work done. The address is 17 Gough Square in London and in fact the house still stands today. It's now a museum called Dr Johnson's House, full of artifacts and publications dealing with Sam generally, but especially focused on the work done there on the dictionary. Now, just as then, the "garret"—that is, the top floor of the house—is the main highlight in this regard. This is where Sam sets up the space where the six men who help him on the project work.

There is a well-known story about Sam being asked about the ambitious deadline by William Adams, his long-time friend, who pointed out that the forty members of the Académie française took forty years to compile their dictionary. "'Sir, thus it is,' Johnson answered playfully; 'this is the proportion. Let me see; forty times forty is sixteen hundred. As three [the number of Sam's helpers varies over the course of the project] to sixteen hundred, so is the proportion of an Englishman to a Frenchman.'"

Though some people often loosely call this the first English dictionary, strictly speaking it is not. It is the first to implement some methods for compiling a dictionary—more about that later—but it is not the first English dictionary of any kind *outright*. That distinction belongs to one published in 1604 called *A Table Alphabeticall* and compiled by a man named Robert Cawdrey.

This is the first *monolingual* English dictionary—that is, the first one in which English words are defined using English words. Many *bilingual* dictionaries were published in the 1500's well before Cawdrey's. We still have these today of course, translating words from foreign languages into English, and vice versa.

But even the claim of Cawdrey being the first is debatable, or at least needs to be qualified a little, because he relies extensively on a dictionary published about a decade earlier. Edmund Coote's book *The English Schoole-Maister*, published in 1596, includes as an appendix a list of words mostly derived from Latin and French, and with a definition in English. Generally, the definition is simply just, as Coote puts it, a "more familiar English word." And another scholar has found a book with an English–English dictionary that was published even before that, in 1530.

We have such easy access to all sorts of dictionaries and definitions these days that it might be difficult to imagine a time when there were no English-language dictionaries at all, or at least none that gave definitions of everyday words. The subtitle of Cawdrey's *Table Alphabeticall*—a bit clarifying, a bit sexist—reads in part: "Conteyning and Teaching the True Writing and Understanding of Hard Usuall English Wordes… Gathered for the Benefit & Helpe of Ladies, Gentlewomen, or Any Other Unskilfull Persons." (In later printings and editions, the mention of ladies and gentlewomen was omitted.)

Note the word *hard*. One of Sam's main innovations in his dictionary is that it doesn't define just hard words that people might meet in print but otherwise not know the meaning of, but it also contains everyday words as well—a combination of focuses which we expect now from modern-day dictionaries. The other innovation is perhaps even more important, and helped to establish his dictionary as an invaluable resource: he illustrates the definitions with quotations featuring words in use and in context by other writers. Illustrative quotations are one of the main ways in which today's most authoritative dictionary, the *Oxford English Dictionary*, demonstrates when a word was first used in print and how the meanings have changed over time—but Sam's practice in the mid-eighteenth century was the first.

His opinion of the purpose of a dictionary also changes over the course of his compiling it. When he first proposed the dictionary, he thought that "the chief intent of it is to preserve the purity and ascertain the meaning of the English idiom." That's how he describes it in his *Plan* for the dictionary in 1747. By the time the dictionary is actually published in 1755 though, he has changed his attitude towards language and lexicography. In the preface he compares his former desire to stop the language from changing to the faith that some people put in an eternal-youth potion:

> When we see men grow old and die at a certain
> time one after another, from century to century,
> we laugh at the elixir that promises to prolong

life to a thousand years; and with equal justice may the lexicographer be derided, who being able to produce no example of a nation that has preserved their words and phrases from mutability, shall imagine that his dictionary can embalm his language.

This is a huge shift in attitude, from thinking that the so-called "purity" of the language is something that should be preserved—or something that ever existed at all—to accepting and embracing change.

Sam's method of compiling the dictionary systematically is simple and practical. His basic idea is that the correct and current definitions of words are to be found in how those words are used by the greatest writers. And he defines the period he will cover as roughly between the late 1500's and the late 1600's, though he makes some exceptions. He supplements his own library of books on the top floor of his house with other books he has borrowed, and starts reading. He also hires six assistants (often referred to as *amanuenses*) to help him with the transcription. His basic method is simple: as he reads, he underlines each word he wants to include in the dictionary, writes the word in the margin of the book, and puts a line at the beginning and end of the quotation he intends to include to illustrate the use of the word. The assistants then take the books, write the word and quotation on a slip of paper, and arrange the slips alphabetically, making them ready for Sam to prepare the definitions. He used hundreds of books but only thirteen survive to give us insight into Sam's methods.

Sam is behind in his deadline but a lot of work does get accomplished by both him and his assistants. They are essentially finished by May 1754 and the printing of the book proceeds. Just in the last few months before the actual publication, Sam considers the possibility and the advantage of obtaining an honorary degree so that it could be mentioned on the title page of the dictionary. In 1738, sixteen years earlier, he approached both Oxford University and Trinity College Dublin, about the prospect, but was refused by both of them.

Now though he has a more substantial literary reputation—he is a well-known man of letters in London and beyond—and he smartly writes a letter to Thomas Warton, a poet and professor, who is also his friend, to see if Warton could help him in the cause. The printing of the dictionary proceeds and Sam waits anxiously during the late fall of 1754 and early winter of 1755 to hear back, because he has instructed the publisher to hold off on the printing of the title page. Finally, success and relief in February 1755 when Sam hears back from Warton and the actual diploma arrives, a master's degree from Oxford. Sam is thrilled.

So the dictionary is published April 15, 1755—alas, about nine years after Sam committed to the publishers that it would be done in three. The biggest factor in such a spectacular missing of a deadline is not so much Sam's laziness (as he often over-chastises himself for) or the fact that he is a working writer and has other projects to devote himself to as well (notably the twice-weekly *Rambler* essays during 1750–1752)—but really the impossibility of estimating how long a book such as this would take. When he signed the contract, he had nothing to compare the book to *exactly*, and in any case he also had plans to do something different from what other dictionary makers had done. The dictionary is two large folio volumes with a total of more than 2,500 pages. It becomes the authority that people cite on words and their meanings well into the nineteenth century, but there are some quirks and oddities—and mistakes—in it that have become part of the lore about the book over the past nearly three centuries.

Some are words for which Sam provides a personal or opinionated definition. We rightly assume that a lexicographer would not "insert" himself or his life into a dictionary and that he would be strictly objective about the meanings he provides. Sam is mostly like that, but there are a few examples where he allows his personality and opinions to come out. He defines his own occupation, *lexicographer*, for example, as "a harmless drudge." Some of his personal insertions are less sarcastic. For example, in the definition of the word *lich* ("a dead carcase") he also not only includes a brief description of his birthplace of Lichfield—where, mistakenly, he thinks the *Lich* refers to Christians who died as martyrs there—but also includes what we might call today a *shout-out* to the city by including the Latin phrase *Salve magna parens*, meaning "Hail, great mother." *Salve magna parens* is a quotation from the Roman poet Virgil and it was also later adopted as the motto on the coat of arms of the city, as a tribute to Sam's tribute!

Other words are ones which have extremely specific meanings. These are words which have simply dropped away from common usage over the centuries—the English language is of course always in flux, meanings changing, words being added and "disappearing"—or they were words that were "hard" words which were even fairly rarely used during the eighteenth century. The list is long. Few readers have likely read a book with the word *consopiation*, meaning "the act of sleeping," or *viduity* for "widowhood." One of the oddest is *anatiferous*, an adjective which Sam defines as "producing ducks" and then provides an explanation involving barnacles and trees—which of course to the modern reader is no explanation at all. The modern authority on the language, the *Oxford English Dictionary*, clarifies things by explaining that it used to be believed that barnacles grew on trees and turned into geese when they dropped into the water below, or even that the goose in fact grew on the tree by its bill.

Sam's dictionary contains not only *words* that are obsolete, but *meanings* as well—words that we still use today but not in the senses that they were used three centuries ago. *Amazement* is "extreme dejection" and a *librarian* is "one who transcribes or copies books." And there are two forms of publication that got their start in the eighteenth century and whose definitions demonstrate that.

A *novel* is "a small tale, generally of love"—they have changed a lot since then—and the other one is *magazine*, which means in Sam's time more or less what it still means today, but he begins the definition with "of late," signalling this new medium also by referring to the *Gentleman's Magazine*, where he worked when he first arrived in London.

The dictionary goes through several editions even in Sam's lifetime. He is finishing off a revised fourth edition in 1772 which is ultimately published in March 1773. It continues to have enormous influence even after his death, partly due to the innovation he brought to its compilation. But antiquated ideas about what a proper dictionary should be, and how the English language should be tamed, also continue as a kind of counter-force into the nineteenth century. These ideas exist with Jonathan Swift, who writes in 1712 (*before* Sam's dictionary) that "I see no absolute Necessity why any Language would be perpetually changing," and his proposal to keep it from changing was to model the Académie française: "a free judicious Choice should be made of such Persons, as are generally allowed to be best qualified... should assemble at some appointed Time and Place, and fix on Rules by which they design to proceed."

This idea is thankfully never acted on but even after Sam's dictionary there is a "hardening of attitudes to language" that continues into the nineteenth century, even including Sam's counterpart, so to speak, in the

United States, Noah Webster. Part of Webster's idea for a dictionary for English in America is political. "It was very important with a new country to ensure that it was different from Britain." Webster publishes his first dictionary in 1806, *A Compendious Dictionary of the English Language*. In the preface, he is very critical of Sam's admittedly imperfect dictionary-making practices. He cites specific words even, and says in general: "Dr. Johnson was certainly one of the brightest luminaries of English literature; and whenever correctness depended on his own mind, as in ethics, for example, he seldom made a mistake." But as for the compiling of the dictionary, Webster criticizes Sam for simply copying others when there was some gap in his own knowledge, and in some cases where he "fell into mistakes." He concludes finally that "no original work of high reputation in our language, in which so much is well executed, contains so many errors and imperfections, as his dictionary."

There's another anecdote associated with the dictionary that has to be told, because it shows a lot about Sam as a person and scholar, and the state of publishing in the eighteenth century. When Sam's *Plan* for the dictionary was issued in 1747 it was dedicated to Lord Chesterfield (Philip Stanhope, fourth Earl of Chesterfield), and in the intervening eight years Chesterfield does nothing to support Sam in his work. However, when the dictionary is about to be published, Chesterfield publishes two letters in consecutive weekly issues of a periodical called *The World* in which he praises Sam's work, but in that insincere, sycophantic, and pompous manner of someone who doesn't really believe what he is writing about:

> I hereby declare that I make a total surrender of all my rights and privileges in the English language, as a free-born British subject, to the said Mr. Johnson, during the term of his dictatorship. Nay more; I will not only obey him, like an old Roman, as my dictator, but, like a modern Roman, I will implicitly believe in him as my pope, and hold him to be infallible while in the chair; but no longer.

Sam's reaction to the letters is masterful: intelligent and calm, but also clear and direct in its criticism. This is one of the most famous letters that he ever wrote:

> I have been lately informed by the Proprietor of The World that two Papers in which my Dictionary is recommended to the Public were written by your Lordship. To be so distinguished is an honour which, being very little accustomed to favours from the Great, I know not well how to receive, or in what terms to acknowledge.

> When upon some slight encouragement I first visited your Lordship I was overpowered like the rest of Mankind by the enchantment of your adress, and could not forbear to wish that I might boast myself Le Vainqueur du Vainqueur de la Terre [the conqueror of the conqueror of the world], that I might obtain that regard for which I saw the world contending, but I found

my attendance so little incouraged, that neither pride nor modesty would suffer [allow] me to continue it. When I had once addressed your Lordship in public, I had exhausted all the Art of pleasing which a retired and uncourtly Scholar can possess. I had done all that I could, and no Man is well pleased to have his all neglected, be it ever so little.

Seven years, My lord have now past since I waited in your outward Rooms or was repulsed from your Door, during which time I have been pushing on my work through difficulties, of which it is useless to complain, and have brought it at last to the verge of Publication without one Act of assistance, one word of encouragement, or one smile of favour. Such treatment I did not expect, for I never had a Patron before.

The shepherd in Virgil grew at last acquainted with Love, and found him a Native of the Rocks. Is not a Patron, My Lord, one who looks with unconcern on a Man struggling for Life in the water and when he has reached ground encumbers him with help? The notice which you have been pleased to take of my Labours, had it been early, had been kind; but it has been delayed till I am indifferent and cannot enjoy it, till I am solitary and cannot impart it, till I am known, and do not want [need] it.

I hope it is no very cinical asperity not to confess obligation where no benefit has been received, or to be unwilling that the Public should consider me as owing that to a Patron, which Providence has enabled me to do for myself.

Having carried on my work thus far with so little obligation to any favourer of Learning I shall not be disappointed though I should conclude it, if less be possible, with less, for I have been long wakened from that Dream of hope, in which I once boasted myself with so much exultation, My lord, Your Lordship's Most Humble, most obedient Servant,

S.J.

This is a kind of writing that I really admire, and frankly that is hard to achieve successfully. It gives the appearance of being casual in a certain way, and has the flow of a regular letter, but just as the anger is controlled, so are the rhetoric and the phrasing.

Perhaps the best complete online version of the dictionary is *Johnson's Dictionary Online*, which is based on the first (1755) edition. It provides not only the full text of each definition, but also links to an image and to the whole page from the 1755 edition, as well as providing other links to put the definition in context. *Samuel Johnson's Dictionary of the English Language 1756: Online Edition* is less reliable. It simply provides partial definitions from the dictionary, contains errors that seem to be the result of the technical conversion of the text, and also makes it unclear whether it's the 1755 or the 1756 edition that is represented. Finally, a good accessible selection from the dictionary is *Johnson's Dictionary: A Modern Selection*. The words and definitions are selected and edited by scholars, and the book is available in print and ebook versions.

All of these are listed in the Bibliography under *Johnson, Samuel*.

DIGRESSION
Some Words from Sam's Dictionary

This is a small sample of some of the words and definitions, or parts of definitions, from Sam's dictionary, divided into five categories. All may be found in *Johnson's Dictionary: A Modern Selection*.

- Words with Personal or Opinionated Definitions
- Words That Sam Doesn't Know the Meaning Of
- Funny or Unusual Words and Definitions
- Words with Highly Specific Meanings
- Words Showing How Meaning or Spelling Has Changed

They illustrate not only Sam's personality—and that he never hesitated to subjectively insert his personality here and there—but more importantly the fact that all languages change. In some cases, there are words which have very specific meanings which might in fact be useful, but the meanings of these words would be a mystery to most people seeing them these days.

Words with Personal or Opinionated Definitions

excise. A hateful tax levied upon commodities, and adjudged not by the common judges of property, but wretches hired by those to whom excise is paid.

fortuneteller. One who cheats common people by pretending to the knowledge of futurity.

lexicographer. A writer of dictionaries; a harmless drudge, that busies himself in tracing the original, and detailing the signification of words.

patron. One who countenances, supports or protects. Commonly a wretch who supports with insolence, and is paid with flattery.

Words That Sam Doesn't Know the Meaning Of

etch. A country word, of which I know not the meaning.

(The *Oxford English Dictionary* gives this word as a contraction of *eddish*, which is "grass … which grows again" or "the stumps or lower parts of the stalks of wheat or other grain left in the ground by the sickle or reaping-machine." *Eddish* doesn't appear in Sam's dictionary.)

minnock. Of this word I know not the precise meaning. It is not unlikely that *minnock* and *minx* are originally the same word.

(This word does not appear in either the *OED* or in *Merriam-Webster Unabridged*. It does appear in *Wiktionary*, meaning *minnow*, and is described as being related to the same word in Scots. In *Dictionaries of the Scots Language*, it is given as a diminutive form of *minnon*, again meaning *minnow*. It doesn't appear to be related to *minx* at all.)

pastern. The knee of an horse.

(This meaning is just a flat-out mistake by Sam, and is the subject of a funny anecdote. Boswell tells the story: "A few of his definitions must be admitted to be erroneous … A lady once asked him how he came to define Pastern the knee of a horse: instead of making an elaborate defence, as she expected, he at once answered, 'Ignorance, Madam, pure ignorance.'" The pastern is the part of a horse's leg between the hoof and the fetlock; the fetlock is below the cannon and it is the cannon that is below the horse's knee.)

tarantula. An insect whose bite is only cured by musick.

(To say the least, Sam could have bulked out this definition a little. It's not just an insect, it's a poisonous spider. The reference to music calls on the belief that the spider's bite caused tarantism, "a hysterical malady, characterized by an extreme impulse to dance, which prevailed as an epidemic in Apulia and adjacent parts of Italy from the 15th to the 17th century… The dancing was sometimes held to be a symptom or consequence of the malady, sometimes practised as a sovereign cure for it.")

Funny or Unusual Words and Definitions

asshead. One slow of apprehension; a blockhead.

bedpresser. A heavy lazy fellow.

fopdoodle. A fool; an insignificant wretch.

network. Any thing reticulated or decussated, at equal distances, with interstices between the intersections.

(This definition is often cited as an example of Sam obscuring the meaning of a relatively simple word by his own style, preciseness, and choice of words.)

Words with Highly Specific Meanings

adscititious. That which is taken in to complete something else, though originally extrinsick; supplemental; additional.

appetence, appetency. Carnal desire; sensual desire.

to bespawl. To dawb with spittle.

calenture. A distemper peculiar to sailors, in hot climates; wherein they imagine the sea to be green fields, and will throw themselves into it, if not restrained.

deosculation. The act of kissing.

discalceation. The act of pulling off the shoes.

latrant. Barking.

madefaction. The act of making wet.

Words Showing How Meaning or Spelling Has Changed

nocent. (1) Guilty; criminal. (2) Hurtful; mischievous.

ustion. The act of burning; the state of being burned.

CHAPTER 5

WRITING ESSAYS, 1750–1760

SAM IS OFTEN SHORT OF money and sometimes in debt from the late 1740's to the late 1750's, right during the time when he is writing two of the works for which many people know him, even today: his English dictionary and his *Rambler* essays. Being in debt is a serious and much-feared circumstance in eighteenth-century England. People (mostly men) are thrown in prison if their creditors bring legal action against them, and they remain there until the debt is paid. One researcher says that it has to do with the "mind-set of the time." Taking on too much debt "was seen as a form of theft…in a time when…the Old Testament was still a major guide to moral teaching. Theft broke the Biblical commandment, 'Thou shalt not steal.'"

The conditions in debtors' prisons are also pretty appalling. In one called Marshalsea, built likely in the late thirteenth century, a single ward might contain up to fifty men and women in the space of sixteen square feet (about one and a half square metres). The prisoners have to relieve themselves on the floor of the ward and "sickness was endemic." Some die for lack of fresh air in the summer. Sam's friend Richard Savage died in Newgate debtors' prison in 1743. So when Sam is arrested on March 16, 1756, for debt, and taken to a "spunging-house" (a temporary holding place before being sent to prison), he knows that this is serious business. He immediately sends a letter to his friend, the writer Samuel Richardson, who ultimately rescues him by paying the debt.

Sam writes a lot of essays and works for several periodicals during this period. It may be a way of either taking a break from, or procrastinating on, the huge project of compiling a dictionary which he has committed to. The three periodicals to which he contributed the most are the *Rambler* (1750–1752), the *Adventurer* (1753–1754), and the *Idler* (1758–1760).

The twice-weekly essays called the *Rambler* which Sam writes are in some ways his premier work. Sam himself said later in life that "my other works are wine and water; but my 'Rambler' is pure wine." His wife Tetty likes them as well: "I thought very well of you before; but I did not imagine you could have written any thing equal to this," she says to him after the first few essays have been published. They establish Sam's reputation as a moralist in his day, and they provide some fine examples of the kind of writing we now often refer to as "Johnsonian"—stately, balanced, formal in comparison to modern or colloquial English, and often peppered with words that are accurate (he is a lexicographer after all) but well beyond the standard vocabulary of the average reader, in this century or even in the eighteenth.

Yet he is such a skilled writer that he often does not require drafts and re-reading and further revisions in order to get the result he seeks. Ironically, for example, *Rambler* 134 is on the subject of procrastination—and it is written in a hurry, as Sam has put off the task:

> The fine "Rambler," on the subject of Procrastination, was hastily composed, as I have heard, in Sir Joshua Reynolds's parlour, while the boy waited to carry it to press; and numberless are the instances of his writing under immediate pressure of importunity or distress.

The essays are of five main types, and therefore vary in style depending on the type: moral essays, letters from readers, literary criticism, allegories, and tales. It is in the moral essays and to some extent the literary criticism that the writing is stately and formal, and thus often difficult for modern readers to penetrate. The other three types are relatively speaking easier. Of the 208 total, about half are moral essays, a third are letters from readers, and less than one-fifth comprise the other three types.

Sam writes all 208 essays in their entirety except for four of them and parts of three others. I've done calculations in a couple of ways to determine the average length of a *Rambler* essay. These are necessarily approximate, of course, but a typical essay is about 1,500 words long, or about six modern double-spaced typescript pages.

And he does this twice a week. Every writer and reader might have a different opinion, but for me this is an enormous quantity of writing to sustain over two years. The *Rambler* essays, along with Boswell's biography, are probably the source of the most quotations by Sam that people are familiar with these days. The actor David Benson has done a one-man show about Sam as well as recited a small selection of the *Rambler* essays. It's all available on YouTube.

The *Adventurer* is another series of twice-weekly essays to which Sam contributes. The magazine was founded by John Hawkesworth in November 1752, about eight months after Sam published his last issue of the *Rambler*—and it was in fact his admiration for the *Rambler* that was part of Hawkesworth's inspiration. Sam's first *Adventurer* essay is published on March 3, 1753, and over the course of the next year he publishes twenty-nine essays, the last one on March 2, 1754. The essays have some of the "feel" of the *Rambler*, both in their topics and in their style, but they are shorter and *perhaps* a little easier for the modern reader, at least in comparison. Sam also becomes a champion of the magazine and recruits other writers to contribute. He writes to his friend Joseph Warton less than a week after his first essay in the *Adventurer*, and also gives him an idea of what the content of the magazine should be: "They desire you to engage to furnish one paper a month, at two guineas [about £300 today] a paper, which you may very easily perform. We have considered that a Paper should consist of Pieces of Imagination, pictures of Life, and Disquisitions of Literature... I hope this proposal will not be rejected, and that the next post will bring us your Compliance." Sam's plea is not that successful: Warton goes on to write only two essays, early in 1754.

Sam's *Adventurer* essays are still a bit of a challenge to read not only because of his style, but simply also because of the changes that have occurred in the English language since he first wrote them almost three hundred years ago. Here is an excerpt from one of the essays published in 1754 to demonstrate:

> These specious representations of solitary happiness, however opprobrious to human nature, have so far spread their influence over the world, that almost every man delights his imagination with the hopes of obtaining some time an opportunity of retreat. Many indeed, who enjoy retreat only in imagination, content themselves with believing, that another year will transport them to rural tranquillity, and die while they talk of doing what if they had lived longer they would never have done. But many likewise there are, either of greater resolution or more credulity, who in earnest try the state which they have been taught to think thus secure from cares and dangers; and retire to privacy, either that they may improve their happiness, increase their knowledge, or exalt their virtue.

After decades of being exposed to Sam's style and vocabulary, I find these essays understandable but still not without a bit of mental work at figuring out a stylistic flourish or the use of a particular word.

At the end of the decade, Sam becomes involved with yet another periodical, the *Idler* (a supplement to the weekly *Universal Chronicle* newspaper), contributing ninety-one essays over two years, 1758–1760. It is finally in these essays that Sam's style changes noticeably. They are shorter and "lighter," "polysyllabic words, frequent in the *Rambler*, appear rarely," and "the sentences are brief."

Here's an excerpt from one of them:

> Life has no pleasure higher or nobler than that of friendship. It is painful to consider, that this sublime enjoyment may be impaired or destroyed by innumerable causes, and that there is no human possession of which the duration is less certain.
>
> Many have talked, in very exalted language, of the perpetuity of friendship, of invincible constancy, and unalienable kindness; and some examples have been seen of men who have continued faithful to their earliest choice, and whose affection has predominated over changes of fortune, and contrariety of opinion.
>
> But these instances are memorable, because they are rare. The friendship which is to be practised or expected by common mortals, must take its rise from mutual pleasure, and must end when the power ceases of delighting each other.

Notice the short paragraphs and the much simpler language, similar even to the style of modern English.

This decade of Sam's life is more than just writing of course. Once near the beginning and once near the end he has to deal with the deaths of important women in his life, his wife and his mother. Just three days after the last *Rambler* essay is published on March 14, 1752, his beloved but troubled wife Tetty dies at the age of sixty-three. Their marriage, which lasted nearly seventeen years, has been erratic almost during the whole course of it, but Sam is in extreme grief when she finally dies. He is too distraught to make funeral arrangements or even to attend the funeral.

His distress is caused as much by the fact of her death as by his guilt over how good a husband he has been. They frequently didn't live in the same house or even in the same city for months at a time and Tetty drank a lot and became an opium user. Early on in their marriage they stopped having a sexual relationship because she decided she wanted to sleep in a separate bed. Sam was busy writing and trying to manage the family finances (and debt), but they were not behaving as successful marital partners do.

Sam doesn't attribute the decline of the relationship to her alone, in fact sometimes quite the opposite. In prayers he writes on the anniversaries of her death, he expresses much guilt for his own behaviour. On the first one, in 1753, he writes in part simply, "I kept this day as the anniversary of my Tetty's death with prayer

& tears in the morning," but over the years he some-times forgets the anniversary, as naturally the intensity of the grief lessens and he focuses more on memories. He writes this in 1770:

> This is the day on which in —52 I was deprived of poor dear Tetty. Having left off the practice of thinking on her with some particular combina-tions I have recalled her to my mind of late less frequently, but when I recollect the time in which we lived together, my grief for her departure is not abated, and I have less pleasure in any good that befals me, because she does not partake it. On many occasions I think what she would have said or done. When I saw the sea at Brighthelm-ston I wished for her to have seen it with me. But with respect to her no rational wish is now left but that we may meet at last where the mercy of God shall make us happy, and perhaps make us instrumental to the happiness of each other. It is now eighteen years.

Contrast this to the stark comment he makes in a letter to his friend Thomas Warton in 1755, saying that after her death "I have ever since seemed to myself broken off from mankind a kind of solitary wanderer in the wild of life, without any certain direction, or fixed point of view. A gloomy gazer on a World to which I have little relation."

His mother dies in 1759 and in the midst of grief and guilt, Sam also lacks money to pay for the funeral expenses. He quickly writes the short book *Rasselas*, an "Eastern tale" based in Abyssinia, or modern-day Ethiopia. It's a simple story (which we might call a novella today) about a prince who leaves his home in the Happy Valley to see a little of the real world before he inevitably ascends to the throne. Rasselas is accompanied by his sister, her attendant, and a friend who is also a poet. They have various adventures, but the book ends with chapter 49, "The Conclusion, in Which Nothing Is Concluded." Each of the travellers has formed a clear wish for life, but "they well knew that none could be obtained. They deliberated a while what was to be done, and resolved, when the inundation [heavy rain has caused an overflow of the Nile] should cease, to return to Abissinia." The book sells well and the expenses for his mother's funeral are covered.

As with the death of Tetty, that of his mother is also accompanied by much guilt. In both cases it is partly just not having prioritized his time to simply see or be with either of them more often. Sam does get over it, but *before* her death he writes a series of letters to her begging for forgiveness, and *after* her death he makes a similar extreme claim as he did about his wife's death, about his own life in a certain sense being over as well. The letters are sent in a flurry in January 1759 and have the feel of a man trying to ensure that a woman he has loved but neglected receives an overall positive message before she dies:

- "The account which Miss gives me of your health, pierces my heart … Pray send me your blessing, and forgive all that I have done amiss to you."
- "Your weakness afflicts me beyond what I am willing to communicate to you … I know not how to bear the thought of loosing you."
- "You have been the best mother, and I believe the best woman in the world. I thank you for your indulgence to me, and beg forgiveness of all that I have done ill, and all that I have omitted to do well."

Things get better. The 1750's have been an intense decade for Sam. He didn't have much money and even faced the possibility of being jailed for debt. He wrote an enormous amount: essays, the completion of a dictionary, a novella. And though he lost two important people in his life, he is about to meet two more.

The Four Reasons You Are Having Trouble Reading Sam's Writing

The difficulty in reading some of Sam Johnson's writing is not a modern problem. Even back when Sam was still alive, people were poking fun at his writing style, calling it elaborate and nearly impossible to read, though not everything he wrote is difficult to read.

I visited the Samuel Johnson Birthplace Museum in Lichfield, England, in January 2020, and while I browsed the shelves of the bookstore before I made my way out, I overheard a conversation that a couple in about their seventies were having with one of the museum staff. They obviously knew about Sam, but I was struck when the woman talked about the difficulty in reading any of Sam's works because they are written, as she put it, "in Old English."

She didn't accurately mean *Old English* in the same sense that linguists use that term—for linguists, Old English is the form of the language from the fifth to the eleventh centuries, well before Sam was writing—but rather that even in Sam's English seven centuries after Old English and only three centuries before our own, the language is different enough and Sam's writing style is unique enough to make the reading of it often hard slogging even for an educated modern-day reader.

She is fortunate that Johnson *didn't* write in Old English, because it truly would be discouraging:

> Hwæt wē Gār-Dena in geār-dagum
> þēod-cyninga þrym gefrūnon,
> hū ðā æþelingas ellen fremedon.

Which "translates" as:

> So. The Spear-Danes in days gone by
> and the kings who ruled them had courage and
>   greatness.
> We have heard of those princes' heroic
>   campaigns.

What I'd like to do in this digression is to give the main reasons why Sam's language is difficult so that at least you will have those explanations to remind you when you come across a hard part in the writing. At worst they will at least explain why you can't understand the passage—but at best they can help you actually understand it better (or at all!). It may take some time, as it does when one is learning any "foreign" language, but with practice you can develop a facility for it.

Based on my own experience of reading Sam's writing over the course of some forty years, here is what I think slows people down:

1. *The English language has changed.* As I write this in 2023, something I read by Sam could be from 240 to 290 years old. Language changes even over short periods of time, so that words no longer mean the same thing as they did a few years ago. Or they take on new meanings. Look at the word *woke*. It used to mean mostly the same thing it has meant

in English since at least the thirteenth century, that is, the past tense of *wake*. Sam defines it this way in his own dictionary in 1755: "Not to sleep... To be roused from sleep... To cease to sleep." No difficulty there.

But look at what has happened to the word *woke*. It now means something very socially positive or hyper political correctness, depending on your politics and point of view. There is no *woke* in this sense in Sam's dictionary, to say the least.

This is a bit of an extreme example, but my point is that of all the thousands of words that Sam used in his writing, likely hundreds and hundreds of them either have a completely different meaning now, or were used by Sam in a meaning that we don't use the word in any more. In addition, words which are very common to us now were shiny and new when Sam was including them in his dictionary.

So.

The result of all these changes in meaning of so many words is that by the time you are sitting down to read the *Idler* or *Rasselas* a few centuries later, no matter how well they are written, you will bump into words that make you stop. And if there's a paragraph full of such words, you may in fact have no idea what Sam is talking about. Imagine a paragraph of two hundred words where ten words were crossed out and another ten were in German. You could probably power your way through that paragraph, but as you continued and found that the whole text was like that, it might discourage you from reading and drive you toward the television.

I'm not mocking Sam nor being flippant about language change. My point is that it is very understandable why reading Sam can be difficult for the modern reader.

2. *Sam uses "big words."* It may be no coincidence that most of the essays for which he is well known were written while he was compiling his dictionary and a few years afterwards (basically, the 1750's). Just take a look at a small sample of the words in the "Digression: Some Words from Sam's Dictionary" to get an idea of the specificity of vocabulary he was working with.

3. *Sam's writing style*. Many books and articles have been published dealing specifically with Sam's style. What does *style* mean when applied to writing? I think of it as *tendencies* that the writer has, characteristics or methods or even quirks that they use over and over. There are probably cases where the writer is not even aware of the tendencies, but for a skilled writer such as Sam they are intentional. He felt that these were the methods to best get his ideas across. Sometimes the writer, and sometimes readers and literary critics centuries later, might refer to the style as being "natural" to the writer. This doesn't mean natural in the sense that they were born that way, of course, but that the style

becomes a kind of signature, something which readers recognize as typical of the writer.

Sam's style can be a problem for modern readers, and was parodied by some of his contemporaries, but it's important to note that there was much praise for it and for his writing generally even in his own day. A contemporary writer, Anna Seward, who is often called the "Swan of Lichfield" (though she wasn't born there), was a poet about thirty years younger than Sam. She praised his style for its "efflorescence and strength of language"—*efflorescence* meaning blossoming—and preferred it over an "unornamented style." So in a sense she was praising his style for the exact same aspects that can give modern readers so much trouble.

Sam is difficult to read when you don't recognize the style, or when you become immersed in it and get lost, unable to tell yourself, *Oh, I see, I'm in the middle of one of those long paragraphs with elements of style which are not modern. I need to slow down here and recognize the pattern.*

As mentioned, Sam's style has been much studied. I will summarize here some of the most important basics that any first-time (or confused!) reader coming to his writing should be aware of. These are not the full story: I don't want to get into every detail for fear of making this worse by explaining a complex style with a long list of items.

Overall, Sam tends to:

- Use long sentences and paragraphs.

- Use "parallelisms" or symmetrical elements in his paragraphs. Here's an example, where I've put them in ***bold italics***:

> The resentment produced by sincerity, whatever be its immediate cause, is ***so certain, and generally so keen***, that very few have magnanimity sufficient for the practice of a duty, which, above most others, exposes its votaries to ***hardships and persecutions***; yet friendship without it is of very little value, since the great use of so close an intimacy is that ***our virtues may be guarded and encouraged, and our vices repressed*** in their first appearance by ***timely detection, and salutary remonstrances***.

You can see what happens. The basic effect is simply to make the paragraph—in fact this is a single sentence—longer, but the other effect is that the reader is constantly having to process additional information, which can tend to slow you down but also of course requires thinking at some level. That resentment which starts the sentence is not only "certain" but it is "keen." There are not only "hardships" but also "persecutions." And that last part about "virtues" and "vices" has symmetries within symmetries.

This can be a lot to take in and is very different from much modern writing, which tends to be shorter and less structured.

One of the issues that modern readers have with Sam, I believe, is that they often start with what is arguably his most famous but also one of his more difficult writings: the over two hundred essays called the *Rambler* that he wrote twice a week from 1750 to 1752. These are indeed excellent writing and deserve to be read, but they are an example of the "packing" of the hardest aspects of Sam's style all in one essay. Long sentences. A "parallel" or "balanced" practice in those sentences where you have to sometimes go back to the beginning of that long sentence to see what is being paired with what. Abstract and sometimes obscure words. Words which have changed meaning.

4. *Sam uses different words for the same concept.* This is something that many writers and speakers do even today, and Sam was not the one to start it but he certainly did practise it. You see it today when a news reporter starts talking about a fire but eventually calls it a blaze, and typically goes back and forth between the two words. You see it regularly in the way that vaccination was referred to during the COVID-19 pandemic. People get vaccinated, get the jab, roll up their sleeves, and get the shot—and no doubt several other variations that I am not including.

In grammar books and usage guides from a hundred years ago it was called *elegant variation*, though you don't see that term used very often these days. The idea was that those who avoided using the exact same word were more interested in writing "prettily" than "clearly," and the fault was laid on "the advice given to young writers never to use the same word twice in a sentence—or within 20 lines or other limit." It's fascinating that after all this time, apparently many people from meteorologists (snow, the white stuff) to politicians (freedom, liberty) are still unconsciously following the same advice.

Sam also did the same in his writing. And combined with the three other difficulties in understanding some of his writing, it can make for a tough slog for the modern reader. In that same example that I quote above, he uses *sincerity* first and then *intimacy*.

One other thing that should be mentioned about barriers to reading is not unique to Sam and is a small thing, but something a modern reader has to get used to if reading texts that reproduce Sam's printed text exactly. That is the presence of what is called the long *s*. Both the *s* that we are familiar with today and the long *s* were used at the same time throughout the eighteenth century, with the long *s* ultimately falling out of use in the early nineteenth. It looks like an *f* with the horizontal bar missing, as you can see in the illustration. The *s* and the long *s* were not interchangeable: the long *s* wasn't used for a capital *S* and it was never used at the end of a word.

Figure 1. The use of the long *s*. (From *The Beauties of Johnson: Consisting of Maxims and Observations, Moral, Critical, and Miscellaneous* (London: G. Kearsly, 1781), p. 40. The quotation is from *Rambler* 161, originally published Oct. 1, 1751.)

So, in this example, *produces* looks like it would in any current book, but *desires* and *pleasure* do not.

All these things together can combine to keep people away from reading anything by Sam *at all*. This is really a shame and is partly attributable to the popularity of Boswell's biography—Boswell himself was also an excellent writer—where such a lively story is told about Sam's life, and with quotations from letters and other works, that many modern readers feel they really don't need to read the originals, especially if they are a challenge.

So, what are readers to do if they want to read Sam's works? You need a Samcycle with training wheels on it. The two works I would recommend to start with are quite different, but they have one thing in common:

fairly easy to understand and to read through smoothly without being constantly stopped by a word you have never heard of before, or a "Johnsonian" sentence which you might get lost in. One is his novella *Rasselas*, which is also very short, and the other is the series of essays called the *Idler*. These make for pretty basic reading and will give you confidence to take off the training wheels and perhaps attempt the *Rambler* all on your own.

Remember, too, that not all the essays in the *Rambler* are equally dense. In the last issue of the series, Sam divides the essays he has written into four categories:

1. "excursions of fancy"
2. "disquisitions of criticism"
3. "pictures of life"
4. "essays professedly serious"

Categories 1 and 3 might also make for a successful initial foray. And in my own thesis on the *Rambler* I divide these into five more easily recognizable categories and indicate which essays fall into which category. See the work in the Bibliography under my name, and consult pages 45–46.

Finally, there are Sam's letters, some of which are often available in anthologies of his writings or even in "selected letters" collections all on their own. They will give you a taste of his everyday writing, at the same time as you learn a little more about his life as well.

Happy reading.

CHAPTER 6

SHAKESPEARE'S PLAYS, 1756–1765

PLAYS ARE A POPULAR FORM of entertainment in Sam's time. They started to be performed again in 1660 after the Restoration, when King Charles II permitted the performances (after a nearly two-decade hiatus), and the pent-up enthusiasm lasted well into the eighteenth century. The plays written in the first decades after the Restoration are notoriously raunchy, with the theme of the cuckolded husband being very common.

In the early eighteenth century, as the audiences became larger and were made up of regular citizens and not just the wealthy elite, riots among theatre-goers were frequent for various reasons. One scholar has identified four main types of riots—based on politics, the content of the plays, the management of the crowd, and differences in factions attending—and tracked them from 1730 to 1780.

Sam is a fan of the theatre and in 1756 he is between projects. His dictionary was published the previous year and he has nothing to dedicate himself to. A project or an ongoing commitment is always his preference. He doesn't want small things here and there with long periods of free time in between—he is hard enough on himself when he *doesn't* have free time—but rather a big project. These are of two types: one like the *Rambler* essays where he is committed to produce a piece of work twice a week for an indefinite period, or one like the dictionary where a single gigantic effort of scholarship has to be carried through to completion. Sam is organized enough to be a fairly dependable writer when there are regular frequent deadlines. He never missed a single issue of the *Rambler* over two years, though it was a close call sometimes, as in the famous incident with the printer's boy waiting at Johnson's side while he writes and the completed pages go right into the boy's hands and then straight to the publisher. No time or desire to ponder over niceties of phrasing or content, which, frankly, came to him naturally.

Sam is much less dependable with bigger "one-off" projects where the deadline is many months or years away, and procrastination and spending too much time at the club or coffee house make for a bad combination. He signed the contract for the dictionary in 1746 and committed to have it finished in three years. It wasn't published until 1755. Nonetheless a group of publishers, headed by Jacob Tonson, approach Sam this year, 1756, with another huge project: a complete new edition of the plays of William Shakespeare. Sam signs the contract on June 2, and six days later he publishes his *Proposals for Printing, by Subscription, the Dramatick*

Works of William Shakespeare. This is a short publication, just eight pages, in which Sam sets out how he will edit and comment on the plays differently than previous editors have, as well as when and how he plans to publish the book.

It is important to note that the *by subscription* in the title refers to a common way of publishing books in the eighteenth century. It has a different meaning than it does when referring to twentieth- and even nineteenth-century practices. It does not mean, as we commonly use the phrase today, that buyers committed to a subscription as we would to, say, a magazine, and expect to get issues delivered at a regular frequency. Nor does it refer to the nineteenth-century practice for the publication of many novels, in which chapters were published originally in newspapers, and only later all gathered together and sold as a book (Charles Dickens, for example, published many of his novels in this way—the other term used to describe this is *serialization*).

What it means here is that Sam gathered commitments and funds from people who intended to buy a copy of the book when it would be published. It is sort of like what people do on crowd-funding sites these days. They have a project in mind and they post the details on Kickstarter or some other site, offering incentives to backers to donate money to the cause. In Sam's case though, the book *is* going to be published for sure and the search for subscribers is simply an added way of creating publicity—and registering commitment—before the book is actually published and for sale. Alas, there are not many subscribers to the Shakespeare edition. Even a year and a half later Sam confides in a letter to a friend that "the subscription has not been very successful."

In the *Proposals*, Sam sets out the two main reasons he is embarking on a new edition of the plays—as he puts it, "to correct what is corrupt, and to explain what is obscure." The first reason has nothing to do with censoring Shakespeare. What he means is that since the plays were originally published and performed in some cases over 150 years earlier, the text may be corrupted in the sense that changes to Shakespeare's original words may have been made accidentally or on purpose. Someone transcribing to make another copy might make a mistake. Or an actor might intentionally change a word in order to improve it to their taste.

The second reason is obvious and is what people who publish editions of classic works do routinely. With the benefit not only of his own education, but of decades of commentary by others—including other full editions—Sam can explain words or lines or passages in Shakespeare that he judges may not be clear to contemporary readers. The language has changed between Shakespeare's time and Sam's, so some words will be unfamiliar. In addition, Shakespeare used many sources for his stories which the eighteenth-century reader may not know and, of course, as a creative writer in a creative age, he also experimented with language. "These,"

Sam writes in the *Proposals*, "are the principal causes of the obscurity of Shakespeare."

And so Sam starts in at the work of compiling a new edition. He has promised to compare the various original copies of the plays available, but frankly he does not do that comprehensively. The two main categories here are the true originals, that is the quarto versions which were published around the time that each play was first performed (*quarto* referring to a book made up of one or more large sheets that have been folded into four in order to produce eight pages when sliced and trimmed)—and what is now known as the "First Folio," the first published collection of all of Shakespeare's plays in 1623 (*folio* here referring to an unfolded sheet and so producing a book that is taller and wider as a physical object).

Sam frankly does not completely do the scholarly work necessary to compare the different versions—nor the practical *legwork* to track down the copies he needs. He somewhat disingenuously blames this on the unwillingness of men who own copies to lend them to him, but this is not really the case. When the book is eventually published in 1765, he writes in the preface that "I collated such copies as I could procure, and wished for more, but have not found the collectors of these rarities very communicative." One modern scholar says that Sam is too "scrappy" to do the "deeply, deeply methodical" work which is necessary for a Shakespearean editor.

There is an obvious person in London who has one of the best collections of Shakespeare's various plays, and from whom Sam does borrow at least some copies: David Garrick, the now-famous actor and producer, and the young former student who came to London with Sam about twenty-five years earlier. Garrick is by this time also a wealthy man—he has profited both in fame and money from that horse ride with Sam so many years before. Sam is frankly bitter both about this and about the fact that Garrick is "only" an actor, whereas Sam is a scholar trying to elucidate Shakespeare for the masses.

The disdain and anger are obvious in what he tells Boswell when asked about why Garrick is not mentioned in the preface: "I would not disgrace my page with a player. Garrick has been liberally paid for mouthing Shakespeare. If I should praise him, I should much more praise the nation who paid him. He has not made Shakespeare better known. He cannot illustrate Shakespeare. He does not understand him." This is unfair to Garrick, who at least claimed he was very willing to lend copies, even instructing his butler "to let Mr. Johnson have whatever books he wanted; but he never applied for any"—all this in spite of Sam's well-known habit of not treating books as physical objects very well. One result is that Sam's edition relies not so much on those primary-source original copies of the plays, but on previous editors' editions and their commentaries.

Sam procrastinates, or is slow getting the work done, and as with the dictionary, he goes well past the deadline he promised. Part of the reason is his natural way and part of it is his having badly underestimated how long it would take to produce an edition of all the plays. John Hawkins published a biography of Sam just three years after his death, and in it he criticizes him for the delays: "It was provoking to all his friends to see him waste his days, his weeks, and his months so long, that they feared a mental lethargy had seized him, out of which he would never recover." Hawkins is even more frustrated by the fact that in the middle of devoting his time to the lagging Shakespeare edition, Sam agrees to write an essay series called the *Idler* for two years from 1758 to 1760 for the weekly periodical the *Universal Chronicle*. Hawkins comments snarkily in his biography that the title of the column is appropriate since Sam is diverting his time from another commitment which he is apparently neglecting.

Apart from his usual inattention to deadlines, Sam is also held back this time—a little unlike himself—by the real feeling that others in the past have done better scholarly work on Shakespeare than he could either do or want to do. "The real monster he feared was the textual work," one modern biographer says. "He knew there were better Shakespeare editors out there who would censure him for slipshod work, and such a prospect troubled and somewhat paralysed him."

Still, he pushes on and finally on October 10, 1765, *The Plays of William Shakespeare* is published in eight volumes, the subtitle continuing: *With the Corrections and*

Illustrations of Various Commentators, to Which Are Added Notes by Sam. Johnson. Modern scholars generally acknowledge that Sam didn't do enough work on the text of the plays, and certainly not what he promised in his *Proposals* nine years earlier, but that many of his comments in the explanatory notes are very insightful.

One of his notes to *King Lear* has always stuck with me since I first read it decades ago. In his closing comments on the play, Sam writes: "I was many years ago so shocked by Cordelia's death, that I know not whether I ever endured to read again the last scenes of the play till I undertook to revise them as an editor." This detail reveals a lot about Sam's capacity to empathize with the characters in a story as well as his attention to dramatic surprises—here, virtue does not prevail and dies in the end—and also about how he thinks about plays and literature generally. They should not only be well-written literature but they should also follow some rules and even teach some lessons for real life. The scholar Tiffany Stern says that Sam "kind of invented ... character criticism." She means that "he thinks through the Shakespeare characters and he thinks about them sort of as real people ... he thinks Shakespeare is very good at kind of what people are actually like."

It's an attitude that Sam pursues in more detail in the preface to his edition of the plays, where he writes that "the end of writing is to instruct; the end of poetry is to instruct by pleasing." This is a common sentiment among both writers and readers in the eighteenth century: literature should be well written but it should also either teach you something or reaffirm something that you already believe (e.g., that virtue is rewarded). Many people in all centuries, before and after the eighteenth—including our own—felt and feel that way about literary writing. Others, though, emphasize that it is the words, the arrangement of those words, and the overall structure of the literary work that are the most important thing, even the *only* important thing. It doesn't matter about lessons or messages or subject matter. A good example of this kind of writer in modern times is Vladimir Nabokov, author of the famous and infamous novel *Lolita*, about a middle-aged man who has a sexual relationship with a 12-year-old girl. Nabokov defended himself vehemently against the strong criticism of the book by "gentle souls who would pronounce *Lolita* meaningless because it does not teach them anything … *Lolita* has no moral in tow."

But back in 1765 when Sam is writing his preface to Shakespeare, he lays out many details about both the playwright's plays and the editor's work. He praises Shakespeare for his "just representations of general nature," for the natural dialogue of the characters, for his alternation between "seriousness and merriment" in a play, and generally for holding a mirror up to real life. But he has criticisms, too, one of them being the lack of "moral purpose" in the plays, and another being Shakespeare's love of puns (called *quibbles* in the eighteenth century). Sam feels that puns even have a "malignant power over [Shakespeare's] mind" and that they are so irresistible to him that when one occurs to him he basically sets aside the line of thought he is writing on and follows the dancing pun. But overall his assessment of Shakespeare's achievement is extremely positive: only Homer was better at "exciting restless and unquenchable curiosity, and compelling him that reads his work to read it [all the way] through."

Sam spends about the last third of the preface writing about his own method as an editor and discussing the editors who have preceded him, sometimes critically. There is an overall tone of defensiveness to this whole section, in part because he is concerned that his scholarship and especially his editing itself—all the commas and the periods and the comparisons to previous editors and editions—will be found lacking. At one point he outright admits to a lack of rigorous editorial diligence when he is comparing the different editions of the Folios: "I collated them all at the beginning, but afterwards used only the first."

He is also snarky and bitter at times, with a kind of tone that you don't expect in the preface to a major scholarly work. He mocks a previous editor named Lewis Theobald for being too celebratory of his editorial changes—"I have sometimes adopted his restoration of a comma, without inserting the panegyrick in which he celebrated himself for his atchievement"—and then continues to criticize him.

Finally, Sam talks about his practices in his own edition, explaining and making a case for spending time on what the reader might consider mere "trifles" and on the rationale behind the explanatory notes he provides for the text. As he famously puts it: "Notes are often necessary, but they are necessary evils."

And so, finally, his edition of Shakespeare brings to an end another years-long project which Sam committed to (again, long past the deadline, but he does manage to finish). Another achievement during the year is that on July 23, just a couple of months before his Shakespeare is published, he is awarded an LL.D. (Doctor of Laws) degree by Trinity College in Dublin. As one modern scholar notes, it is therefore an *Irish* university which is the first to make him "Dr. Johnson," a title which many people still know and call him by. "It was another sweet reward for decades of labour in his now vanished wilderness of literary and social neglect." He has, so to speak, *arrived*.

For the record, Sam goes on to produce a second edition of the plays, but this time with much assistance from the Shakespearian scholar George Steevens. In fact, Sam contributes very little to the effort, but *The Plays of William Shakespeare in Ten Volumes with the Corrections and Illustrations of Various Commentators, to Which Are Added Notes by Samuel Johnson and George Steevens, with an Appendix* is published in 1773.

CHAPTER 7

SAM AND JAMES BOSWELL, 1763–1784

MANY PEOPLE WHO KNOW ANYTHING about Sam at all know it because of the great biography written by James Boswell. The biography is long but entertaining, with Boswell inserting himself into the story as necessary. He also records in detail conversations, discussions, and other exchanges that Sam has with a wide variety and large number of people throughout the last two decades of his life especially.

Boswell is a fascinating character himself. He was born in Scotland but he prefers life in London, where he likes socializing with men and women of status and wealth. He's a talker, vain but charming, confident and brash, but also insecure. Boswell lives his life under the general disapproval of his father, Alexander, who is both a supreme court judge and the owner of a large estate in Scotland called Auchinleck. James is ambitious in his own way, but he doesn't apply himself as much as his father would like.

Sam and James meet for the first time in 1763 when Sam is in his early fifties and James in his early twenties. Sam is well established as a leading literary man in England, and Boswell is still in search of a career. They meet in a bookshop run by Thomas Davies. Boswell records the details of the iconic meeting in the biography that he would publish about thirty years later:

> At last, on Monday the 16th of May, when I was sitting in Mr. Davies's back-parlour, after having drunk tea with him and Mrs. Davies, Johnson unexpectedly came into the shop; and Mr. Davies having perceived him through the glass-door in the room in which we were sitting, advancing towards us,—he announced his aweful approach to me, somewhat in the manner of an actor in the part of Horatio, when he addresses Hamlet on the appearance of his father's ghost, "Look, my Lord, it comes." I found that I had a very perfect idea of Johnson's figure, from the portrait of him painted by Sir Joshua Reynolds soon after he had published his *Dictionary*, in the attitude of sitting in his easy chair in deep meditation, which was the first picture his friend did for him, which Sir Joshua very kindly presented to me, and from which an engraving has been made for this work. Mr. Davies mentioned my name, and respectfully introduced me to him. I was much agitated; and recollecting his prejudice against the Scotch, of which I had heard much, I said to Davies, "Don't tell where I come from."—"From

Scotland," cried Davies roguishly. "Mr. Johnson, (said I) I do indeed come from Scotland, but I cannot help it." I am willing to flatter myself that I meant this as light pleasantry to sooth and conciliate him, and not as an humiliating abasement at the expence of my country. But however that might be, this speech was somewhat unlucky; for with that quickness of wit for which he was so remarkable, he seized the expression "come from Scotland," which I used in the sense of being of that country, and, as if I had said that I had come away from it, or left it, retorted, "That, Sir, I find, is what a very great many of your countrymen cannot help."

It's a great story and the writing gives a good idea of Boswell's style: accurate and attentive to details, but also lengthy, and with a desire always not to leave anything ambiguous (for example, in his explaining all the ins and outs of how he inadvertently sets Sam up for his quip about Scotland). In spite of Boswell's concern about the poor first impression he makes, Davies tells him that Sam would like to see him again in his chambers. Boswell avails himself of the invitation a few days later, and two weeks later they meet again at the Mitre Tavern in Fleet Street.

Many of the best anecdotes, stories, and quips which we recognize now as quintessential Sam come to us from the journals that Boswell keeps and the intimate, detailed biography that he eventually writes. He describes all aspects of Sam's character and behaviour. Let's start with Sam's way of eating:

> I never knew any man who relished good eating more than he did. When at table, he was totally absorbed in the business of the moment; his looks seemed rivetted to his plate; nor would he, unless when in very high company, say one word, or even pay the least attention to what was said by others, till he had satisfied his appetite, which was so fierce, and indulged with such intenseness, that while in the act of eating, the veins of his forehead swelled, and generally a strong perspiration was visible. To those whose sensations were delicate, this could not but be disgusting [distasteful]; and it was doubtless not very suitable to the character of a philosopher, who should be distinguished by self-command. But it must be owned, that Johnson, though he could be rigidly *abstemious*, was not a *temperate* man either in eating or drinking.

Sam is a man of many passions—intellectual, emotional, and physical—and he certainly enjoys his food and drink. "I mind my belly very studiously and very carefully," he tells Boswell, "for I look upon it, that he who does not mind his belly will hardly mind anything else."

On the other end of the spectrum, Sam talks about philosophy, too, in his own way. Sam, always a common-sense man, rejects vehemently the philosophy espoused by George Berkeley, who is active during the first half of the eighteenth century. Berkeley is a proponent of a philosophy called immaterialism—the "apparent denial of the reality of any external world, with the consequent shrinking of reality down to a world of minds and their own sensations or 'ideas.'" Boswell recounts the story:

> After we came out of the church, we stood talking for some time together of Bishop Berkeley's ingenious sophistry to prove the non-existence of matter, and that every thing in the universe is merely ideal. I observed, that though we are satisfied his doctrine is not true, it is impossible to refute it. I never shall forget the alacrity with which Johnson answered, striking his foot with mighty force against a large stone, till he rebounded from it, "I refute it *thus*."

This is a classic little episode from Sam's life. On the one hand it's the reaction of a practical man who has no time for any of the more abstruse or theoretical aspects of knowledge and philosophy. If matter doesn't exist, then what is all this stuff that I am surrounded by? Sam is a well-educated man—Adam Smith tells Boswell that "Johnson knew more books than any man alive"—and so likely part of him realizes that his so-called refutation is just an extreme and simplistic dismissal of a philosophical stance with some validity in one context or another. On the other hand, Sam can be in fact as categorical as he seems to be, and in many instances he lives up to the caricature of the cranky old man often attributed to him.

Sam and Boswell do become good friends, though Sam also plays the role of the attentive and supportive father that Boswell feels he is missing from his actual father. Boswell idolizes Sam and takes pride and pleasure in his presence, watching him, trying to emulate him. He writes his monumental biography of Sam based to a large extent on their social outings and their private conversations, but Boswell is a very inquisitive fellow as well, and not shy about asking others about details that he isn't directly privy to himself.

One of Boswell's characteristics that he's proud of (and brags about in his journals and in letters to friends—but definitely never to Sam) is his sexual appetite and prowess, spending a lifetime having affairs and especially using the services of prostitutes. He has gonorrhea many times and suffers through the long recuperation that treatment in the eighteenth century demands. Prostitution is not illegal and he avails himself of the brothels and street prostitutes whenever he is in London. A directory of London prostitutes (*Harris's List*) is published annually for the "man of pleasure" such as Boswell.

His biography of Sam and his journals recount many incidents about both men and are the primary source of much information about Sam in many modern biographies (including this one).

DIGRESSION

Sam's Charity

Perhaps one of Sam's most admirable traits is his appreciation for the plight of the underdog, and more importantly his regular efforts and actions throughout his life to help them out. He is not just a spouter of platitudes and nice words about how terrible it is to be poor or outcast or otherwise disadvantaged: he does something about it to the extent that he can. His charity starts, literally, in his home.

One of Sam's modern biographers, Peter Martin, has a good account of the various people who live with Sam for long or short periods of time. The two main people are Anna Williams and Robert Levet. Miss Williams, as she was generally called, is a blind poet. Sam takes her in at times of need first, but eventually she becomes a permanent resident. She often has no money whatsoever. Miss Williams is cranky and doesn't get along with other residents in Sam's home, but she sort of runs the place. The other one is Robert Levet, sometimes called Dr. Levet though he has no formal medical training. He learned about the body and about medications on the continent. "He was not a pretty sight in his mid-fifties when he moved into Gough Square, standing at five-feet five-inches tall, extremely thin, grey, and scarred by smallpox."

There is also Elizabeth Desmoulins, a friend of Sam's wife, Tetty. In 1752 Sam also takes into his house as a servant a black boy and former slave named Francis

Barber (Frank), who is about ten years old at the time. Mrs. Desmoulins (née Swynfen), as she is mostly called, is married to Jacob, who is Frank's teacher before he moves in with Sam. It was "certainly not typical [to take in a black servant]" nor to "leave a major inheritance to any servant." Frank is likely paid more or less what a white servant would be paid.

These are the main regulars, but there are also many for whom Sam provides shelter for a night or two. Except for episodes when Frank runs away for various reasons, he and Sam stay loyal to each other till the end. In 1768 Sam sends Frank off to a grammar school in the town of Bishop's Stortford, about 60 km northeast of London, to get an education. In fact, even when Frank gets married five years later, and still later has a boy they name Samuel, Sam allows them all to lodge at his house.

Frank actually becomes the controversial main beneficiary of Sam's will, receiving £750 (about £115,000 today) to be paid as an annual £70 annuity (about £10,000 today), and then whatever is remaining in goods after other people have been provided for. It all totals over £2,000 (£300,000 today). David Nokes writes that "the publication of the Will caused great consternation, not for the various small bequests of books, but for the large amount bequeathed to the manservant Frank Barber, a black man who had been a slave… That Johnson had… paid for his education and treated him as a friend was widely known;

but to leave him 'an annuity of seventy pounds' was scandalous."

Sam likes and has pets in the house, too, notably always a cat. The best known is Hodge. Penny Taylor, who worked at the Samuel Johnson Birthplace Museum, provides a nice summary of Sam's affection for cats. He has them throughout his life, though the names of only two survive (Hodge and Lily). Sam treats Hodge well, as Boswell reports: "I never shall forget the indulgence with which he treated Hodge, his cat: for whom he himself used to go out and buy oysters, lest the servants having that trouble should take a dislike to the poor creature." There is a statue of Hodge, two empty oyster shells in front of him, just outside Dr Johnson's House in London.

CHAPTER 8

SAM'S FRIENDSHIP WITH HESTER THRALE, 1765–1784

SAM MEETS HESTER THRALE AND her husband Henry for the first time at their home on January 9, 1765. Sam is fifty-five and Hester is twenty-three or twenty-four. (Both her birthday and the year are uncertain, but the latter is either 1740 or 1741.) She's been married to Henry for only about fifteen months and they have a large house and property called Streatham Park (or Streatham Place), and which they generally refer to as simply *Streatham*. It's located about 10 km southwest of London on the other side of the Thames. Streatham Park is a residential suburb of London now, but in the eighteenth century it was greenery—or, as a descendant of Henry describes it, "wholesome, green and rural."

Henry Thrale inherited a successful brewery from his father, as well as property and the house which had been built on it in 1730. Streatham, one of three houses that he owns, is huge. The grounds occupy eighty-nine acres. (To try to put that in a modern perspective so that some readers could make the comparison, eighty-nine acres is about thirty-six hectares—about the size of

2,900 homes of 1,300 square feet [120 square metres] each.) As for the house itself, it is "a fine villa, of white stucco, three stories high… with nearly two miles of gravel paths." It is in a "paddock [field], separated from the park by a lake and drawbridge." A hundred-yard driveway leads from the gates to the front of the house.

The Thrales have sought Sam out as a guest. It's the middle of the week, a Wednesday, during the day, and he is introduced to them by Arthur Murphy, a playwright (mostly) whom Sam has known for about ten years and who has been a good friend to him. As Hester recounts it, Murphy has been a long-time friend of her husband as well and he convinces Henry to invite Sam to his home so that he can witness Sam in conversation. His reputation for talk, both in the clubs and elsewhere, has become a legend in and around London.

Once Henry is convinced, Murphy then suggests an enticement to get Sam to come. They also invite James Woodhouse, who is a bit of a minor celebrity at the time as the "shoe-maker poet," plying a trade by repairing shoes but also publishing poetry—and all before he turns thirty. Sam agrees to come to the dinner but it's dubious that the poet is really the draw. Sam gives him advice during the visit, basically to read the works of Joseph Addison if he wants to be "a good writer, or what is more worth, an honest man."

Over the course of the next twenty years or so, Sam would spend many days and weeks at Streatham, a friend of Henry, admired and tended to by Hester, and liked by the children as well. He becomes almost a part of the family, but he uses some of his time there to escape his busy and messy flat in London so that he can get some writing done.

Streatham also becomes the place he goes, or where Hester insists he stay, during periods when Sam is physically or mentally unwell. The pattern of care starts not long after the first meeting. One biographer writes that around Easter 1766 Sam's physical illness gives way to a "severe mental breakdown." He doesn't leave his home for weeks and he complains that his "horrible" mind is "distracted." When the Thrales visit him in June, they see him at his worst. Hester intervenes directly and immediately, taking him to Streatham, where she takes care of him for a full three months. "Those three months were a turning point in his life. For the next sixteen years he spent much of his time with Mrs Thrale and her husband at Streatham and Southwark [in London, where they also had a house], virtually as a member of the family. His relationship with her became, apart from his marriage to Tetty, the most important one in his life."

The visits and the extended stays that Sam makes at Streatham are by far mostly positive and beneficial for him. He is mostly used to living in a noisy house inhabited by people *he* is doing the favour for, and is often alone late at night in his melancholy. Hester caters to Sam and is attentive to his behaviour and needs. She writes in a book of anecdotes published just over a year after his death:

> Mr. Johnson loved late hours extremely, or more properly hated early ones. Nothing was more terrifying to him than the idea of retiring to bed, which he never would call going to rest, or suffer another to call so. "I lie down (said he) [so] that my acquaintance may sleep; but I lie down to endure oppressive misery, and soon rise again to pass the night in anxiety and pain."… he used to shock me from quitting his company, till I hurt my own health not a little by sitting up with him when I was myself far from well… sit quietly and make tea for him, as I often did in London till four o'clock in the morning.

To her credit, Hester tolerates a lot with Sam. He is the same irascible, opinionated, and categorical talker in the civilized domesticity of the Thrales' home as he is in the various clubs where he would dominate discussion, and often cares very little for the people he crushes in argument. But even though he is cranky and seemingly dissatisfied with meeting and dealing with people there, he gets to converse and he gets to debate, which are two of his favourite activities.

Things change over time in the household, regarding not only Sam but also Hester and Henry. Their wedding was one that Hester resisted (she wanted to be a writer), but she ultimately gave in to pressure from her mother and other family members to marry the wealthy Henry in 1763. The couple have twelve children, but eight of them die young, and there are miscarriages as well. "For fifteen years Hester was almost constantly pregnant," one scholar writes. Making things worse is that in 1778, around the time of her final pregnancy, she is convinced that her husband is having an affair, and writes in her diary:

> Mr Thrale is fallen in Love *really* & *seriously* with Sophy Streatfield [Sophia Streatfeild]—but there is no wonder in that: She is very pretty, very gentle, soft & insinuating [subtle, ingratiating]; hangs about him, dances round him, cries when She parts from him, squeezes his Hand slyly, & with her sweet Eyes full of Tears looks so fondly in his Face.

It's obvious from her flat tone that she is not much bothered by another woman being in love with a man she herself has never really loved. She has supported him though, even six years earlier when Henry's mismanagement of the brewery from which he derived his fortune was threatened with bankruptcy. His friend Humphrey Jackson convinced him that it would be possible to brew beer *without malt and hops*. It failed, of course, and Henry turned to Hester, Sam, and his chief clerk John Perkins to get things back in order. They found credit for the brewery, and Hester convinced a "near [mutinous]" group of brewery workers to work with her, as they refused to work for Henry's benefit.

This arrangement continued more or less until Henry's death on April 4, 1781.

Hester inherits the brewery and promptly sells it for a large fortune, £135,000 (about £20,000,000 today). She and Sam remain friends and Sam still has access to Streatham Park. At least for a few more years. It's worth noting that at Streatham there is only Hester and her children now. Sam and Henry have become good friends over the course of the fifteen years since they met, and Henry's death affects Sam deeply. It is not a peaceful death and Sam is there because he has been called to come. The night before Henry was "in high spirits… and coming home, he wolfed down an enormous dinner, with strong beer 'in such quantities!' as Hester noted, that 'the very servants were frighted.' That meal finished him." Sam is a witness to his final hours in the early morning.

DIGRESSION
Sam's Sexual Life

The fact is that not a lot is known for certain about Sam's sexual life and not a lot has been written about it in biographies, books, articles, and other scholarly sources. And just to be clear: I'm not writing about it here for sensationalist or prurient reasons. I'm not prying to "dig up dirt" or to discuss anything puerile. But I also know that Sam was a man of passions for many things in life—eating, port, tea, debating, morals, God, friendship—and even the little that scholars have found out or speculated on suggest a man with a strong sexual passion as well. And sex being an important aspect of most people's lives, an incomplete picture of Sam is drawn if his sexual life is not included as well.

Let's start with the basics. He was born in 1709 and there's no evidence to suggest that he had sex with anyone before he got married in 1735. That marriage lasted till 1752, when his wife Tetty died, and Sam was then in his early forties. Even during the marriage, there were long and frequent periods during which the couple lived in different cities, and Tetty also drank and took opium, beginning a "slow and gradual decline" as early as 1740.

There are some facts and famous anecdotes that are known about his sexual life, especially during his marriage, but the period during which he was a widower—more than half of his adult life—is mostly the territory of obscure and ambivalent details and some occasional speculation by scholars.

One well-known story relating to Sam and Tetty took place during the time when he (ultimately unsuccessfully) ran a school at a rented farmhouse called Edial Hall for about a year during 1735–1736, "about two and a half miles [4 km] west of Lichfield in a tiny rural crossroads in the middle of nowhere." One of his students was David Garrick, who would later leave Lichfield with Sam for London and become a highly successful actor, director, and producer. At the school, the boys spied on Sam. His "oddities of manner, and uncouth gesticulations, could not but be the subject of merriment to them; and, in particular, the young rogues used to listen at the door of his bed-chamber, and peep through the key-hole, that they might turn into ridicule his tumultuous and awkward fondness for Mrs. Johnson."

I've always found the stark contrasts in this famous story—this *image* really—very sad and moving. The ungainly young man, intelligent, fairly newly married to his already fading older wife, the school day over and he is driven by the same primal passions that move most of us. The students defy their teacher in a casual invasion of privacy, with even Garrick showing disrespect and disregard.

Sam did have a fondness for smart and beautiful women, but of course there is nothing in such attraction that doesn't apply to a wide swath of men, especially as the age gaps widen. Another slightly funny, slightly confessional anecdote relating to Sam and sex is his statement to Garrick about why he couldn't hang around behind the stages: "I'll come no more behind your scenes, David; for the silk stockings and white bosoms of your actresses excite my amorous propensities." That's the sanitized version that Boswell published in his biography, but an earlier draft phrases it as it really was: "For the white bubbies and the silk stockings of your actresses excite my genitals."

Beyond these scattered details, which don't present a broad picture so much as five-second tidbits, some scholars have done research to try to uncover something more substantial about Sam's sexual character and behaviour. One of the earliest is Katharine C. Balderston, who in 1949 proposed a highly controversial conclusion about Sam's sexual life during part of the time when he was friends with Hester Thrale, that is, mostly in the late 1760's and early 1770's, when Sam was in his early sixties. She looked a little more closely than others had at not only entries in Thrale's diary and in letters between her and Sam, but also at a padlock and note handwritten by Thrale which were part of the sale of her personal effects after her death in 1821. The note read: "Johnson's padlock, committed to my care in 1768."

The scholar's conclusion was that Thrale and Sam had a sadomasochistic relationship. He liked to be confined by her to his room, shackled, and whipped or beaten. This was partly the fulfillment of an erotic fantasy caused by his suppression of strong sexual desires after his wife's death.

Sixty years later, another scholar, Jeffrey Meyers, built on Balderston's research and proposed that a Latin phrase tacked onto the end of Sam's diary entry for March 31, 1771 (Easter, by the way) refers to and explains the padlock: "De pedicis et manicis insana cogitatio," which he translates as "insane thoughts about foot-fetters and manacles." And the final piece of this theory concerns an exchange of letters between Sam and Thrale in 1773, in one of which Sam complains about not being enslaved enough, and she chides him for "quarrel[ling] with your Governess for not using the Rod enough."

As you might imagine, this theory has been strongly criticized and outright rejected by many modern scholars. One of them suggests that Sam's big secret is not sexual masochism but rather masturbation, which Sam tracked but disguised with the simple annotation "M" in his diaries (another suggests that Sam was tracking his defecation schedule). Many clergymen and medical quacks in the eighteenth century believed that the "self pollution" of masturbation could drive you insane. This scholar suggests that Sam couldn't control his sexual desire, and so instead of committing the sin of masturbation, he asked his friend Hester Thrale to do it for him. (This strikes me as a bit of a technicality, as if the God that Sam believed in wouldn't realize what he was *really* up to.) And, finally, yet another modern scholar considers the masturbation theory unacceptable and the masochism theory "discredited."

It is telling that this scholar and most others dismiss or underplay the primal and sexual side of Sam. Meyers criticizes some of his peers for their diffidence and even their unwillingness to accept a fact about Sam for which there is good evidence. He writes in part:

> Despite the overwhelming evidence of Johnson's darkest secret, his modern biographers have not been able to reconcile his obsession with their exalted image of the great moralist and stern philosopher. Preferring to keep Johnson safely on a pedestal, they've consistently refused to face the implications of Balderston's discovery... Biographers, like lawyers, should be required to take a course in evidence. I believe Johnson's secret life adds to rather than detracts from his greatness. It makes his character more complex and tormented, his struggle more extreme, his achievement more impressive.

I agree with this assessment.

There are also less dramatic theories and evidence for how Sam managed his sexual life without access to Tetty as a partner. Around the late 1730's, Sam and Tetty are living apart. He is in London but she is in Hampstead, about 10 km northwest. Boswell manages to extract from Elizabeth Desmoulins, who lived with Tetty, that when Sam would visit, he'd call Desmoulins to his bed because he was aroused, and she would get in bed with him, where they fondled and kissed. Though apparently not to consummation: "He'd push me from him and cry, 'Get you gone.'" Boswell remarks that she "saw the struggle and the conquest" as Sam brought himself "to the very verge of what he thought a crime." In effect, Sam gets what satisfaction he can without actually having sex with her.

Another aspect of Sam's sexual life is his fidelity to his wife Tetty. She was a lonesome widow and Sam was a young, inexperienced, but passionate young man when they got married. But the later circumstances of life—some necessary (such as Sam moving away to London to get a job), and some the result of Sam being busy and sometimes living apart from her even when they were both living in London—in part led to Tetty's eventual sad decline into anesthetizing herself with alcohol and opium. She becomes unavailable to Sam in more ways than one, and Sam is tempted by other women, tempted by infidelity.

Boswell is very careful and discreet in his recording of what can only be summarized as Sam's adultery. Here are the exact words in his biography:

> On that account, therefore, as well as from the regard to truth which he inculcated, I am to mention, (with all possible respect and delicacy, however,) that his conduct, after he came to London,

and had associated with Savage and others, was not so strictly virtuous, in one respect, as when he was a younger man. It was well known, that his amorous inclinations were uncommonly strong and impetuous. He owned to many of his friends, that he used to take women of the town to taverns, and hear them relate their history. In short, it must not be concealed, that, like many other good and pious men, among whom we may place the Apostle Paul upon his own authority, Johnson was not free from propensities which were ever 'warring against the law of his mind,' [Romans 7:23]—and that in his combats with them, he was sometimes overcome.

So Sam was not perfect. Boswell, not so much defending Sam's actions as explaining and contextualizing them, later quotes Sam himself in saying that "a man may be very sincere in good principles, without having good practice."

In the end, of course, it is difficult to know what the truth is. It could be either of those theories and it could be neither, and some 250 years later the evidence either way is ambiguous. It is the contrast of details in each of the theories that I find compelling and pitiable and sad. Johnson the learned and accomplished writer and scholar either expiating his guilt by way of physical punishment, or reduced to keeping track of his episodes of masturbation so as to monitor and try to prevent his possible slide into madness. In a better world, there wouldn't be such self-punishing guilt, and human sexuality wouldn't be fraught with such ridiculous myths and fears. Or, at the very least, a literate but troubled man who gave so much of his imagination and his scholarship wouldn't have to drag himself through such awful personal torture.

Sam may have written about his actions himself, but in the last days of his life he burned a diary and other papers which he evidently didn't want posterity to know about. One scholar speculates that "the burnt diary probably contained references to his darkest secrets: fear of insanity, lustful fantasies, sexual passions, marital infidelity, masturbation, chains and whips." We'll never know.

CHAPTER 9

A LONG TRIP TO SCOTLAND WITH BOSWELL, 1773

THE HEBRIDES ARE AN ARCHIPELAGO of some five hundred islands in the Atlantic Ocean on the western side of the most northerly tip of mainland Scotland. People usually refer to the Inner and Outer Hebrides, that is, the ones closest to and farthest from the shore. Some of them are still today uninhabited, just as they are in 1773 when Sam and Boswell take a trip there together that ends up lasting more than three months over the summer and fall. Sam is sixty-three years old and Boswell is thirty-two when they start the trip, but they both celebrate birthdays en route.

Sam leaves London August 6 to head to Edinburgh to meet up with Boswell, and they both depart the eighteenth on the first leg. It's a bit incredible to me that with several authoritative original sources, and even more authoritative scholarly biographies, the exact details of the route that Sam and Boswell take are not identical in all sources. This is likely in part due to some writers wanting to indicate every single stop of their itinerary, others leaving out some stops or conflating them, and perhaps the occasional error.

The *general* route is easily stated though. They do a basic circular route, starting and ending in Edinburgh; go along the eastern shore of Scotland as far north as Aberdeen; travel west across the northern part of Scotland as far as Raasay; head south to Coll; and then make their way southeast back to Edinburgh. Depending on the lay of the land or sea, they go "by coach, horseback, foot and boat," and "of their actual travelling time, more was spent in the islands than on the mainland." Norman Page provides a detailed itinerary, including their modes of travel. See the simple illustration on page 131.

It isn't till three full months later, on November 9, that they are finally back at the Boswells' home in Edinburgh. Sam stays there for a while, visiting various people in and near the city, but mostly spending the night at the house. On November 21 he and Boswell travel to Blackshiels in the evening, and the next morning, November 22, 1773—about three and a half months after Sam set out from London—the friends part, Sam taking a coach back to the city. They have travelled about 1,100 km in total together. Both men write books about their trip, though separated by ten years in publication. Boswell waits until 1785 to publish his, a year after Sam's death—*The Journal of a Tour to the Hebrides*—but Sam starts writing his version in the spring of 1774.

It is in his *A Journey to the Western Islands of Scotland* that Sam initiates a public battle between himself and a Scottish writer named James Macpherson over what comes to be known as the "Ossian fraud." Sam has already expressed his view personally to Boswell and others that Macpherson's supposed translations into prose of poems by a supposed third-century Gaelic poet named Ossian are fakes. And he is right. "Macpherson invented most of the *Ossian* canon himself, even though he did occasionally draw on oral and manuscript sources of extant Gaelic ballads." In the *Journey* Sam is categorical: "I suppose my opinion of the poems of Ossian is already discovered [known]. I believe they never existed in any other form than that which we have seen. The editor, or author, never could shew [show] the original; nor can it be shewn by any other."

The *Journey* is published on January 13, 1775, and two days later Macpherson writes to the publisher, William Strahan, asking that the offending words about him be removed in future editions. Strahan actually visits with Sam to try to convince him to do so, and in the end the words of the first edition remain. This infuriates Macpherson enough that he apparently writes a letter to Sam (which, unfortunately, has not survived the centuries), that causes this now-famous reply on January 20:

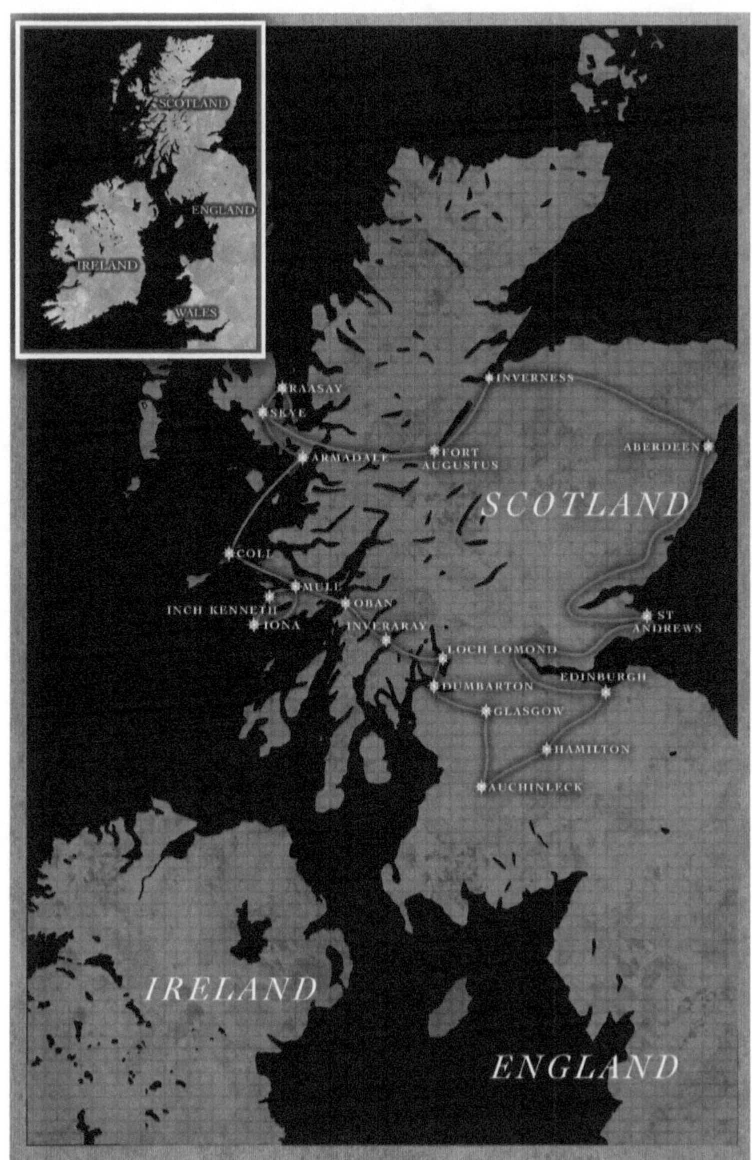

Figure 2. Itinerary of the trip to the Scottish Hebrides that Sam and Boswell took in 1773. *(Daniela Cordero, original map, 2023)*

Mr. James Macpherson—

I received your foolish and impudent note. Whatever insult is offered me I will do my best to repel, and what I cannot do for myself the law will do for me. I will not desist from detecting what I think a cheat, from any fear of the menaces of a Ruffian.

You want me to retract. What shall I retract? I thought your book an imposture from the beginning, I think it upon yet surer reasons an imposture still. For this opinion I give the publick my reasons which I here dare you to refute.

But however I may despise you, I reverence truth and if you can prove the genuineness of the work I will confess it. Your rage I defy, your abilities since your Homer [a translation of the *Iliad*] are not so formidable, and what I have heard of your morals disposes me to pay regard not to what you shall say, but to what you can prove.

You may print this if you will.

In the end, nothing comes of the dispute—nobody gets into a fight, either physically or legally—and subsequent editions of Sam's *Journey* continue to include the debunking of Macpherson's work.

CHAPTER 10

WRITING SHORT BIOGRAPHIES OF ENGLISH POETS, 1777–1781

ON MARCH 29, 1777, THREE booksellers (publishers) meet with Sam and offer him a proposal. The three of them, along with thirty-nine others as well as six printers, have formed a consortium to publish a collection of English poetry, and they want Sam to write a short biography and critique of each of the poets. Sam doesn't decide that day, but ultimately agrees to the consortium's terms. After the upcoming book is advertised and noticed by Boswell, he asks Sam in a letter to tell him more about *The English Poets, with a Preface, Biographical and Critical, to Each Authour, by Samuel Johnson, LL.D.* Sam replies on May 3 that indeed he has "engaged to write little Lives, and little Prefaces, to a little edition of the English Poets."

Sam starts to work on the biographies in the summer but (typically) he doesn't follow strictly what the publishers have asked him to do. The main issue is that in many cases Sam expands the "little Lives" into fairly lengthy biographies. The longest is of Alexander Pope, at over two hundred pages; the shortest, Richard Duke, a mere two pages and only about three hundred words. The first volumes of the *Lives* are published in March 1779 and the last ones in May. They vary not only in the length and detail that Sam dedicates to each poet, but also in his opinion of each of his biographical subjects.

His biography of Jonathan Swift, author of many varied works during his life but most famously *Gulliver's Travels* (1726), is often negative and dismissive. Right from the start when he mentions that Swift was born in England but also lived in Ireland, and so alternately called himself English or Irish, Sam is snarky: "The question may, without much regret, be left in the obscurity in which he delighted to involve it." Whatever Swift's motives in calling himself one or the other, it is the biographer's job to decide the facts or at least provide some speculation. Swift wasn't "delighting" in not nailing down one or the other, but was likely emphasizing his English roots whenever there was the chance that someone in power would notice and so post him to an important position in England. And in the end Swift gave up on his dreams of English "preferment," as it was called, and lived mostly (and died) in Ireland.

Sam is a more conservative writer than Swift, who was a hardcore satirist, and so he characterizes *A Tale of a Tub* (1704), arguably Swift's best book, as "wild" and even "dangerous," though he also singles it out as unlike anything else. Sam is right though about Swift's misguided idea to "fix" the English language by establishing an academy to oversee usage. Sam's experience in actually making a dictionary taught him that this is neither possible nor recommendable. The biography continues like that, with Sam in a very workman-like way making his way through Swift's life and writings, and in the end he concedes that Swift has borrowed from very few writers: "in all his excellencies and all his defects [he] has so well maintained his claim to be considered as original."

There is not room to go through all the individual *Lives*, and I give this one as an example of where Sam doesn't hesitate to criticize or show his biases, but also calls out excellence where he finds it. The other fifty-one biographies show a similar balance.

Perhaps the best known of the writers whom Sam covered in the *Lives* are:

- John Milton, 1608–1674
- Samuel Butler, 1613–1680
- John Dryden, 1631–1700
- Jonathan Swift, 1667–1745
- William Congreve, 1670–1729
- John Gay, 1685–1732
- Alexander Pope, 1688–1744
- Richard Savage, 1697–1743
- Thomas Gray, 1716–1771

The rest, whatever their literary accomplishments, are generally known only to academics and specialists who study the era or the particular poet. Even though their works may no longer be popularly known today, Sam's achievement in the *Lives* is a major biographical work. Three years later Sam works on a revision, with assistance and additions by the printer and writer John Nichols, the Shakespeare scholar George Steevens, and the ever-present James Boswell. Sam finishes the last of the revisions at Hester Thrale's Streatham estate in September 1782, and the second edition is published in 1783.

DIGRESSION
Sam's Lifetime of Letter Writing, 1731–1784

The latest authoritative edition of Sam's correspondence contains about 1,500 letters that he wrote between 1731 (when he was twenty-two years old) and 1784 (three days before his death at seventy-five), as well as documentation for another approximately 175 letters that he is known to have written but which have not survived the years. That doesn't mean of course that those were absolutely all the letters he ever wrote: these are just the ones that scholars know about.

By far the person that Sam wrote the most letters to was Hester Thrale. In the nineteen years they were friends, from 1765 to 1784, Sam wrote about 385 letters to her, more than twenty percent of all the letters he wrote to all his correspondents.

Another important fact to remember is that of course Sam did not write the same number of letters every year. There is only the one in 1731, to Gregory Hickman, a distant relative. And in 1784, the year he was ailing and ultimately died, he wrote over 190 letters, more than one every two days on average.

I've always also been interested in the signatures on Johnson's letters: how he signs his name. The vast majority (over ninety-nine percent) of the letters are signed *Sam: Johnson*, with his first name abbreviated with a colon. It doesn't matter who the correspondent is, new friend or old, business or family member, early in his life or when he is older—it's almost always *Sam:* (with the colon). In fact, there are *only six* letters of that entire total that are signed in some other way: one as *S.J.*, two as *Saml: Johnson*, and three with his full name, *Samuel Johnson*. (Note: that latest edition of Sam's letters renders the colon as a period for some reason.)

It's interesting to note that the letter signed with the least amount of information and the least indication of personal engagement—just a spare *S.J.*—is the famous one to Lord Chesterfield, in which Sam is venting his dislike and disrespect for Chesterfield's lack of support for him as he did the hard work of compiling his dictionary. Chesterfield made himself visible only after the dictionary had actually been published, praising Sam in a very insincere, artificial, and pretentious manner. Sam's letter was written on February 7, 1755, just a couple of months before the dictionary was published.

Sam remembered this negligence on the part of Chesterfield in at least two of his other publications as well. In his poem "The Vanity of Human Wishes," first published in 1749, one of the lines detailing the many bad things about life is "Toil, envy, want, the garret, and the jail." But in later editions Sam changed *garret* (meaning the top floor of a house, an emblem of the kind of place an unknown writer might toil away without notice) to *patron*. And in the dictionary itself, Sam defines *patron* in part as "One who countenances, supports or protects. Commonly a wretch who supports with insolence, and is paid with flattery."

Some grudges are never forgotten.

Another one of Sam's notable correspondents was Dr. Richard Brocklesby. Sam sent him only twenty letters, but nineteen of those were during the four months preceding his death. Brocklesby became a trusted and knowledgeable professional to whom Sam could confide his worsening ailments and ask for advice. Sam knew that he wasn't getting any better and so in a sense the letters serve as another kind of journal of his decline, with the occasional respite. "I am loath to think that I grow worse," he wrote on July 31, 1784, "and cannot fairly prove even to my own partiality that I grow much better." The subsequent letters set out in some detail his ailments:

- loss of strength
- trouble sleeping
- "asthma" (Sam referred to it by this term but it was likely emphysema produced by chronic bronchitis)
- difficult, painful urination
- weak legs and limbs
- dropsy (accumulation of water in the body)
- constipation

The letters to Brocklesby also refer to his medications and other treatments:

- tincture of cantharides (dried Spanish-fly beetles)

- dried squills (an onion-like plant) combined with vinegar
- opium (and opiates)
- diacodium (an opiate made from the heads of poppies)
- infusion of wood ashes
- fasting
- drinking milk
- castor (plant) oil

The last letter Sam ever wrote is much more mundane than the depressive and dispiriting ones he wrote to Dr. Brocklesby. It is to William Strahan, one of the many publishers he had worked with during his life, and the man who had printed Sam's dictionary. The letter is dated December 10, 1784, just three days before Sam's death, and he is basically asking that whatever allowance of funds is due to him be sent. The letter reads in full:

> I am very unwilling to take the pains of writing, and therefore make use of another hand to desire that I may have whatever portion of my pension you can spare me with prudence and propriety. I am, Sir, your humble servant,
>
> Sam. Johnson

"Another hand" likely refers to someone who transcribed what he dictated. It's a bit sad that his last letter involves asking for money, especially during a time when he himself likely realized that he was dying.

CHAPTER 11

SAM'S SICKNESS AND DEATH, 1781–1784

SAM IS FAIRLY ACTIVE DURING most of 1781, but this is also the year when his illness, which will affect him fitfully and ultimately lead to his death, really begins. For much of the year he is engaged in activities that are very familiar and usual for him. His relationship with the Thrales continues and they are generous toward him as they have always been since they first met. They are wealthy enough not only to have the huge mansion in Streatham Park, but also a place in Southwark in the city of London, about 10 km north. When they move to a different house within the city, they make sure that "a room is assigned" to Sam.

He also continues his typical life of visits, reading, writing, dining with friends, and going to church. Sam sees a wide variety of people and his itinerary reads almost as it would in any previous active year. He even accompanies Boswell for part of the trip when he returns home to Scotland. On June 2 and 3, among other activities, they visit others along the way and visit a church in Welwyn. On June 3, "they go to Southill Church, and after dining at Dilly's house drink tea with the Vicar of Southill." The next day they visit the country house of Lord Bute—and it's not until the fifth that Sam parts from Boswell, and makes his way back to London.

Sam is a little sick and has a few ailments during the latter half of 1781, but it's not until the beginning of 1782 that things become seriously worrying. One scholar says that this year is not the start of a "slow decline" but rather "a ferocious battle with a variety of disorders." Boswell summarizes: "his complaints increased, and the history of his life this year, is little more than a mournful recital of the variations of his illness."

The year starts with an emotional jolt unrelated to his sickness. His long-time friend Robert Levet, whom he met in 1746 and who actually lived in Sam's house full time for the last twenty years of his life, dies on January 17 at the age of seventy-six or seventy-seven. Levet practised medicine, mostly for poor people, but he had no formal training and no medical license. In the eighteenth century, "medicine was largely unregulated and it was not uncommon for people to set themselves up as 'doctors' without any specific medical qualifications." Such doctors fulfilled an important role for the poor of the era. "They couldn't afford the physicians at the time, who would charge a guinea or half a guinea for a consultation... So they went to someone in the village who had got together a reputation for knowing how to deal with illnesses... And these people, it turns out, had developed quite a following." (One guinea would be worth about £150 today.)

Sam writes an elegy on Levet's death but it's not published until August 1783 in the *Gentleman's Magazine*. It's warm and praiseful, and defends his friend for practicing his "single talent" (medicine). Here is part of it:

> See Levet to the grave descend;
> Officious [kind], innocent, sincere,
> Of ev'ry friendless name the friend.
> Yet still he fills affection's eye,
> Obscurely wise, and coarsely kind;
> Nor, letter'd arrogance, deny
> Thy praise to merit unrefin'd.

Sam is alternately sick, and then better for a while, and then sick again, for the rest of 1782. He does manage to at least try to carry on life as he always has, but the logistics are tougher (for him and for his friends) and the periods of sickness combined with the frequent inability to get a good night's sleep just drag him down. He undergoes bloodletting several times, and takes opium when he wants to ensure that he sleeps through the night. His rooms in Bolt Court are still his home, but he is several times rescued by Hester Thrale to spend time in more comfort at Streatham, where she can also take care of him as needed. In a relatively healthy period in June he goes to Oxford for about a week and a half, but his motivation is more a "change of air" and "to catch at the hope of better health" than the city or the people he might see. Later in the year he manages to get some work done as well, specifically finishing the final work for a revised reprinting of his *Lives of the Poets.*

The year 1783 continues in the same pattern of the previous year, but with the bouts of illness not only more frequent but also more intensified and debilitating. Sam's mind is still good but his body is obviously starting to fail him. Often it is during the nights when he suffers, in pain and unable to sleep. Boswell says that in spite of that, Sam still maintains "the same ardour for literature, the same constant piety, the same kindness for his friends, and the same vivacity both in conversation and writing." One of those friends is Boswell himself, who is in London for about ten weeks from March to May, and visits Sam several times, often coming away concerned about his condition. But Sam appreciates the company and the conversation.

As the year rolls on, though, he starts to feel the sadness and depression of solitude and loneliness. He has always had a house full of lodgers who could talk with him or provide entertainment or distraction. But now Levet is dead, his regular lodger Mrs. Desmoulins has moved out because of her constant arguments with Miss Williams, and even Frank Barber and his wife have left as well. Then while visiting his friend William Bowles at his estate near Salisbury, he hears word that Miss Williams has died on September 6. She was ailing when he left for the trip and so it's a lonely home in Bolt Court in London that he returns to. Sam is heartbroken; he has known her for over thirty years, and she lived in his home for most of that time. Boswell says that "her peculiar value was the intimacy in which she had long lived with Johnson, by which she was well acquainted with his habits, and knew how to lead him on to talk." In a letter to his long-time friend Bennet Langton two weeks after her death, Sam confides how much he valued her: "I have lost a companion, to whom I have had recourse for domestick amusement for thirty years, and Whose variety of knowledge never was exhausted." (He means *amusement* not in the sense of humorous entertainment but rather pleasure derived from an interesting person.)

This year of loss and illness—which included a minor stroke, a tumour, gout, and even problems with a tooth—comes to an end with a little bit of hope. He's a couple of months past his seventy-fourth birthday, but still intellectually and physically active. He decides that what he needs in his life is another discussion club to attend, and so he forms the Essex Head Club, named after the pub in which the meetings are to take place every Monday, Thursday, and Saturday evening.

Sam hopes for better results from this club than he had in the previous month's effort to revive the old Ivy Lane Club from over thirty years ago. He and a couple of the former members of that club did have one meeting, but the ambience was a little too placid for Sam. They talked about being old, and the evening not only was too "tender" and "melancholy," but they just had a meal, finished up with coffee, and broke up early to go home. It wasn't the robust conversation and debate well past midnight that Sam was used to and preferred.

Things go well for the first couple of meetings, but on or around the night of the third meeting, Saturday, December 13, Sam becomes sick. One source says that he actually suffers a coronary thrombosis (a clot inside one of the blood vessels of the heart). In any case this is his last Essex Head meeting for the next couple of months, as the illness is serious enough to keep him out of commission. It's not just the result of eating too much food and having a little too much to drink. He is actually laid up at home for months at a time, not going out to *any* club or *anywhere*, and in pain. He gets better, then relapses, and the sad cycle recommences and continues.

This will be a year filled with horrible illness and heartbreak. Starting the day after the thrombosis he is confined inside until April 21, almost four full months. Boswell is back in London on May 5 and visits Sam first thing the next morning. The visit is brief because Sam is headed off to Islington (about 10 km northeast of the city) to stay for a while with his friend George Strahan. Boswell writes that he is "greatly recovered" and heading to Strahan's house "for the benefit of good air, which, notwithstanding his having formerly laughed at the general opinion upon the subject, he now acknowledged was conducive to health." Sam and Boswell see each other frequently during the nearly two months that he is in London.

On July 2, the same day that Boswell leaves London to return home to Scotland, Sam receives a letter from Hester Thrale, beginning a sad and devastating exchange of letters which ultimately puts an end to their nearly twenty-year friendship. And the fact is that Sam, during his months of sickness, when he sought company whenever he could, when he got outdoors and even travelled out of London when he had reprieves, and also when he continued his correspondence with Thrale and complained of her not replying—the fact is that Sam was the cause of the break due to his narrow-minded disagreement with her life plans and his harsh and categorical way of writing to her about it all.

The letter that Sam receives is a version of one she has already sent to several other people, telling them of her intention to marry Gabriel Piozzi, the Italian man who has been giving singing lessons to her daughters for the past three years. It states clearly and openly for the first time that when he gets back from Italy, "his return would be succeeded by our Marriage."

Thrale is extra careful in sending this to Sam, partly because she held this news back from him while others knew, but mostly because she fears his reaction. And so she adds an additional cover letter to explain herself, which reads in part:

> Our Friendship demands somewhat more, it requires that I shd beg your pardon for concealing from you a Connection which you must have heard of by many People, but I suppose never

believed ... I only tell it to you now, because all is *irrevocably settled*, & out of your power to prevent ... & tho' perhaps [I am] the most independent Woman in the World—I feel as if I was acting without a parent's Consent—till you write kindly to your faithful Servt.

Alas, Sam's response two days later is the opposite of kindly. Here it is in full, fueled likely by a combination of emotions, including jealousy, being left out of a secret, considering Piozzi to be socially beneath her, and genuine disapproval of the fact that she would be marrying a Catholic:

Madam: July 2, 1784

If I interpret your letter right, You are ignominiously married, if it is yet undone, let us once talk together. If You have abandoned your children and your religion, God forgive your wickedness; if you have forfeited your Fame [reputation], and your country, may your folly do no further mischief. If the last act is yet to do, I, who have loved you, esteemed you, reverenced you, and served you, I who long thought you the first of humankind, entreat that before your fate is irrevocable, I may once more see You. I was, I once was, Madam, most truly yours,

Sam. Johnson
I will come down if you permit it.

Hester's response on July 4 is frank and strong, and with more grace and understanding than Sam has shown. She asserts her right to marry whomever she wants to:

> I have this Morning received from you so rough a Letter, in reply to one which was both tenderly & respectfully written, that I am forced to desire the conclusion of a Correspondence which I can bear to continue no longer ... To hear that I have forfeited my Fame is indeed the greatest Insult I ever yet received, my Fame is unsullied as Snow ... Farewell Dear Sir, and accept my best wishes. You have always commanded my Esteem, and long enjoy'd the Fruits of a Friendship never infringed by one harsh Expression on my Part ... but till you have changed your Opinion of Mr. Piozzi—let us converse no more. God bless you.

It is in effect the end of an intimate friendship, and it comes in the midst of an illness that only temporarily gets better but then relapses. As if he realizes that what lies ahead is even worse, on perhaps the exact same day when he receives the letter he begins a diary which he calls "Aegri Ephemeris" (July 6), generally referred to as his "Sick Man's Journal." It's mostly in Latin, but overall it "notes his medical condition each day ... whether he slept well ... his bowel movements and the quantity of urine discharged, balancing this against his intake of fluids; his drugs, their quantity and discernible effects."

He maintains the journal for a full four months and during that period, externally, it might appear as if his life is normal. He goes to church. He has visitors and writes letters. Sam even travels—a trip encompassing Oxford, and Birmingham, but mainly his birthplace in Lichfield and in some of the nearby towns where he knows people. It's the same story as before: he is well for a while and delights in that, but very soon he has symptoms again of his many ailments. His last departure from Lichfield is on November 10 and he is back home in London on the sixteenth.

Sam realizes what is happening to his body, its inexorable deterioration, and where this is all soon headed. It has affected him emotionally before, but now he talks even more about depression over the sorry state that he is in. John Hoole visits him about a week later and finds him "extremely low and dejected." As he leaves, Sam says, "I am very poorly indeed!" And it's the same thing on December 3 ("extremely low") and the 8th ("very poorly and low").

It is around this time that Sam realizes that he has written down some personal details that he does not want to be revealed to others and to posterity after his death. He burns masses of his papers, including letters and especially a detailed diary of his life. Sam is partly motivated by simple anger in some cases, as with the letters from Hester Thrale (*Piozzi* since her July 23 marriage as a Catholic): he burned many but not all and some survive to this day. The diary is a different story, and biographers and scholars from Boswell to the present day lament Sam's action, depriving them of a wealth of information available nowhere else. Some speculate that he confided his darkest thoughts and actions to that diary, but they, and I, and you will never know.

Near the very end, though, he confides to Hawkins (who would go on to write one of the first full biographies of Sam) that even in the midst of pain and debilitation, as his basic activities are curtailed, he is settled with God. This is no small thing for Sam, because he has spent a lifetime berating himself for never quite measuring up to what he thought God wanted from him. Hawkins visits him on November 28, when there happen to be other friends visiting as well, and Sam is asleep. When he awakes he admits that "the prospect of his dissolution was very terrible to him," but he later continues with an extraordinary and overall happy conclusion:

> I have, at times, entertained a loathing of sin and of myself, particularly at the beginning of this year, when I had the prospect of death before me; and this had not abated when my fears of death have been less; and, at these times, I have had such rays of hope shot into my soul, as have almost persuaded me, that I am in a state of reconciliation with God.

But there is no *physical* recovery this time. The same pattern of better, then sick again, persists over the next couple of weeks. By December 12 he is not eating nor taking his medicine, and the next morning the swelling in his legs is so bad that Sam uses a lancet and a pair of scissors to cut them. The day gets worse from there, even though there are many visitors throughout. Hoole comes for a while but finds him "lying very composed in a kind of dozing: he spoke to nobody … he seemed not to take the least notice of any present."

Later, his last words, as he wakes briefly from dozing, are "iam moriturus," Latin meaning "now I am about to die." It is about 7:15 p.m. on Monday, December 13, 1784.

Sam's funeral is held a week later and he is buried at Westminster Abbey in the Poets' Corner, near the statue of Shakespeare and the grave of David Garrick, his life-long friend who accompanied him when they both left Lichfield for London almost fifty years before.

NOTES

PREFACE

- **of twenty-one years** Radner, p. 358.
- **all I have** Nabokov, *Letters*, p. 381.
- **readily perceived symmetry** O'Flaherty, p. 524.
- **a coherent organization** Jones, p. 47.
- **is always coherent** Jones, p. 48.

INTRODUCTION

- **penance was expiatory** Boswell, *Life*, p. 1033.
- **after her death** Page, p. 6.
- **the first place** Reade, part I, p. 1.
- **general were going** Reade, part VI, pp. 59–60.
- **careers in London** Nokes, p. 52; Page, p. 5; Martin, p. 141.
- **acts of piety** Johnson, *Dictionary Online*, "Expiatory. adj.," https://johnsonsdictionaryonline.com/1755/expiatory_adj.

CHAPTER 1

- **a brave boy** Johnson, *Yale*, vol. 1, *Diaries*, p. 3, http://www.yalejohnson.com/frontend/sda_viewer?n=106841.
- **eyesight (almost blind)** Johnson, *Yale*, vol. 1, *Diaries*, p. 5, http://www.yalejohnson.com/frontend/sda_viewer?n=106841.
- **suspicion to him** Johnson, *Yale*, vol. 1, *Diaries*, p. 7, http://www.yalejohnson.com/frontend/sda_viewer?n=106841.
- **of his family** Johnson, *Yale*, vol. 1, *Diaries*, p. 7, http://www.yalejohnson.com/frontend/sda_viewer?n=106841.
- **and got married** Nokes, p. 8.

- **landowners in Birmingham** Piozzi, *Anecdotes*, 1st ed., pp. 12–13.
- **at the time** Martin, p. 13. For the estimate of the population of Cubley, I am grateful to Maxwell Craven, who writes in an email, basing his information on Edwards, pp. 25–26: "This reveals 26 households taxable (and none exempt) from which you might be able to project a total. I think standard practice is to assume an average of four per household, which would yield a very approximate total of 104 souls to which an indeterminate number of waifs and strays probably need to be added, probably rounding up to around 120."
- **for his relations** Johnson, *Yale*, vol. 1, *Diaries*, p. 6, http://www.yalejohnson.com/frontend/sda_viewer?n=106841.
- **Sam also inherited** Reynolds, vol. 2, p. 257; quoted in Martin, p. 17.
- **of around 3,000** "Lichfield"; Lichfield City Council, "Statistics."
- **northwest and Ireland** Lichfield City Council, "History."
- **four years old** Johnson, *Yale*, vol. 1, *Diaries*, p. 23, http://www.yalejohnson.com/frontend/sda_viewer?n=106841.
- **without definite occupation** *Oxford English Dictionary: OED*, "lounge," (verb, def. 3).
- **it, living lazily** Johnson, *Dictionary Online*, "To Lounge. v.n.," https://johnsonsdictionaryonline.com/1755/lounge_vn.
- **from their business** Boswell, *Life*, pp. 91–92.
- **the parchment factory** Martin, p. 58.
- **known come there** Boswell, *Life*, p. 100.
- **to my tutor** Boswell, *Life*, p. 101.
- **now call insensitivity** Boswell, *Life*, p. 101.
- **and all authority** Boswell, *Life*, p. 107.
- **commoners in hall** Martin, pp. 76–78.
- **away with indignation** Boswell, *Life*, p. 108.
- **scholars ever accomplish** Boswell, *Life*, p. 106.
- **made existence misery** Boswell, *Life*, p. 102.
- **its baleful influence** Boswell, *Life*, p. 103.
- **full foot shorter** Meyers, *Johnson*, pp. 2, 214.
- **to the eye** Boswell, *Life*, p. 118.
- **body include giant** Meyers, chap. 4 title, "Benevolent Giant."
- **giant and stout** Burney, p. 225; quoted in Martin, p. 466.

- **he gets older** Boswell, *Life*, p. 118.
- **are deeply visible** Boswell, *Life*, p. 118.
- **they leave scars** *Oxford Concise Medical Dictionary*, "scrofula n."
- **all hid beholders** Piozzi, *Anecdotes*, 1st ed., p. 297.
- **wearing a wig** Boswell, *Life*, p. 118.
- **surprize and ridicule** Martin, p. 119.
- **chewing the cud** Martin, pp. 457–458.
- **in perpetual motion** Martin, p. 466.
- **with a smile** Boswell, *Life*, pp. 316–317; quoted in Martin, pp. 325–326.
- **all in combination** Murray.

CHAPTER 2

- **place in Birmingham** Boswell says that Sam was a guest of Hector and that Hector was a lodger. This implies that Sam, as we might say today, *stayed at Hector's place*, which Hector happened to be renting from the owner, Thomas Warren, publisher of the *Birmingham Journal*: "Being now again totally unoccupied, he was invited by Mr. Hector to pass some time with him at Birmingham, as his guest, at the house of Mr. Warren, with whom Mr. Hector lodged and boarded," *Life*, p. 112.
- **of it survives** See Clifford, *Young*, p. 340, note 41, and Nokes, p. 39.
- **and profitable publication** Boswell, *Life*, p. 113.
- **seen by Johnson** Boswell, *Life*, p. 113.
- **paid 5 guineas** The book was likely published in December 1734 (Page, p. 4), and as was common practice at the time, the place of publication is given as London instead of the actual Birmingham to give the book more cachet (Meyers, p. 56).
- **finds Sam forbidding** Boswell, *Life*, p. 118.
- **wigless; convulsive tics** Boswell, *Life*, p. 118.
- **in my life** Boswell, *Life*, p. 118.
- **first husband's death** Boswell, *Life*, p. 118.
- **his early twenties** See Boswell, *London Journal*.
- **use of cordials** Boswell, *Life*, p. 120.
- **to produce them** Martin, p. 114.

- **church services again** St Werburgh's Church.
- **of the marriage** Nokes, p. 48.
- **who is remarrying** Holloway, *Game of Love*, p. 12.
- **are quite different** Barclay.
- **and Sam do** Barclay.
- **be in tears** Boswell, *Life*, p. 118.
- **some young ladds** Letter from Henry Greswold to Gilbert Walmesley, Aug. 30, 1735, quoted in Reade, part VI, pp. 29–30.
- **the original three** For estimates of the highest number of students Sam might have had, see Nokes, p. 49 and p. 49, note 29.
- **by Samuel Johnson** *Gentleman's Magazine* (June 1736), p. 360. The same ad also appeared in the July issue, p. 428.
- **and correctest authors** Martin, p. 124.
- **at the ceiling** Piozzi, *Anecdotes*, 1st ed., p. 146.
- **protest not eatable** Piozzi, *Anecdotes*, 1st ed., p. 150.
- **rind of resentment** Piozzi, *Anecdotes*, 1st ed., p. 145.
- **in that sense** Carlson; *Oxford English Dictionary: OED*, "magazine, n." sense 6b.
- **to a fault** See senses 1a and 2a in the *Oxford English Dictionary: OED*, "defect, n."
- **where to reply** Johnson, *Letters*, vol. I, pp. 5–6.
- **is not hired** Wain, p. 71.
- **is 8.6 million** UK Office for National Statistics.
- **and 650,000, respectively** Porter, p. 361.
- **less than 100,000** Olsen, p. 57; Porter, p. 363.
- **75 in 1790** Martin, p. 14, note 15; White, *London*, p. xxi; Official Data Foundation; Statista; National Archives.
- **£ 200 a year** White, *London*, p. xxi.
- **modern-day underwear** I am indebted to Savage, Telephone interview, for the information about clothing.
- **five years old** Dr Ben Jackson.
- **was dirty again** Savage, Telephone interview.
- **women or children** Raven.
- **wooden printing press** Raven.
- **to a text** Clayton, Email interview.
- **arbiters of taste** Clayton, Email interview.
- **they saw fit** Peifer, pp. 351–353.

- **the eighteenth century** I am indebted to Frans De Bruyn for background information about copyright and pirating.
- **by September 14** Great Britain, *Calendar*.

CHAPTER 3

- **life can afford** Boswell, *Life*, p. 681.
- **gets a break** Nokes, p. 48; Martin, p. 140.
- **except for money** Boswell, *Life*, p. 591.
- **of the Annotator** Johnson, *Letters*, vol. I, p. 13.
- **John, a librarian** Kaminski, p. 69.
- **with the work** Boswell, *Life*, p. 141.
- **Fairs in Feb.** *Gentleman's Magazine*, Jan. 1731, p. 1.
- **at the magazine** See the *Gentleman's Magazine*, Mar. 1738, p. 156; Martin, p. 153.
- **toward simple "accuracy"** Hessell, p. 167.
- **an explicit byline** "*The Life of Father* Paul Sarpi, *Author of the History of the* Council of Trent: *For Printing a New Translation of Which, by* S. Johnson, *We Have Publish'd Proposals,*" *Gentleman's Magazine*, Nov. 1738, pp. 581–583.
- **known and "notorious"** Holmes, p. 1.
- **about her claim** Sherbo.
- **the following year** Davies; Johnston.
- **an "invisible" one** Holmes, p. 35.
- **the Prime Minister** Kaminski; quoted in Holmes, p. 34.
- **history occasionally interspersed** Johnson, *Yale*, vol. 20, *Johnson on Demand*, pp. 77–78, http://www.yalejohnson.com/frontend/sda_viewer?n=112225; quoted in Martin, p. 214.
- **volume in 1745** Martin, pp. 214–215.
- **the tardy bust** Johnson, *Yale*, vol. 6, *Poems*, p. 99, http://www.yalejohnson.com/frontend/sda_viewer?n=107813.
- **call'd on me** Johnson, *Yale*, vol. 6, *Poems*, p. 215, http://www.yalejohnson.com/frontend/sda_viewer?n=107814.
- **and so on** De Bruyn.
- **pensive discontented temper** Johnson, *Dictionary Online*, "Melancholy. adj.," https://johnsonsdictionaryonline.com/1755/melancholy_adj.
- **of gloomy wretchedness** Boswell, *Life*, p. 86.
- **recover my spirits** Boswell, *Life*, pp. 315–316.

- **scholar puts it** Vickers, p. 10.
- **and coffee houses** Wilson.
- **begun this morning** Johnson, *Yale*, vol. 1, *Diaries*, pp. 257–258, http://www.yalejohnson.com/frontend/sda_viewer?n=106841.
- **help of God** Johnson, *Yale*, vol. 1, *Diaries*, pp. 5–6, http://www.yalejohnson.com/frontend/sda_viewer?n=106841; quoted in Tankard, p. 231.
- **you forsaken me** *Bible*, Mark 15:34.

CHAPTER 4

- **as Dictionary Johnson** See Clifford.
- **of the project** Clifford, p. 54.
- **to a Frenchman** Boswell, *Life*, p. 168.
- **any kind outright** Lynch, p. 142.
- **well before Cawdrey's** Simpson.
- **familiar English word** For an excellent discussion of both Coote and Cawdrey, see McConchie, pp. 103–113.
- **meaning the skyes** Read, p. 188.
- **the English idiom** Johnson, *Yale*, vol. 18, *English Language*, p. 29, http://www.yalejohnson.com/frontend/sda_viewer?n=106842.
- **makes some exceptions** Martin, p. 236.
- **prepare the definitions** Martin, p. 236; Lynch, p. 145.
- **how he proceeded** Lynch, p. 145.
- **Sam is thrilled** Reddick, pp. 77–78.
- **of the trees** See Mills, "Lichfield," and Institute for Name-Studies, "Lichfield." *Lich* derives from Celtic and Old English words meaning grey, in reference to the colour of the trees.
- **to Sam's tribute** Lichfield City Council, "Civic Insignia." The phrase is from Book II of Virgil's *Georgics* poem.
- **by its bill** See the definitions of *anatiferous* and *barnacle* (n²) in the *Oxford English Dictionary: OED*.
- **design to proceed** Swift, *Proposal*.
- **States, Noah Webster** Thorne.
- **different from Britain** Cotter.
- **as his dictionary** Webster, p. xix.
- **but no longer** Chesterfield.
- **obedient servant, S.J.** Johnson, *Letters*, vol. I, pp. 94–97.

- **or reaping-machine** *Oxford English Dictionary: OED*, "eddish," "etch."
- **Madam, pure ignorance** Boswell, *Life*, p. 222.
- **cure for it** *Oxford English Dictionary: OED*, "tarantula," "tarantism."

CHAPTER 5

- **shalt not steal** Savage, "The Georgian Way."
- **in the summer** White, pp. 46–48.
- **prison in 1743** Holmes, p. 227.
- **is pure wine** Rogers, p. 6.
- **Tetty liked them** Boswell, *Life*, p. 179.
- **have been published** Piozzi, *Anecdotes*, 1st ed., p. 48.
- **of three others** Jones, pp. 4–5.
- **over two years** The two calculations I did were to average the texts as given in the Project Gutenberg versions of vols. 1 and 2 at https://www.gutenberg.org/files/43656/43656-0.txt and https://www.gutenberg.org/files/11397/11397-8.txt, respectively; and to do the same for the Kindle version of the complete *Rambler* essays at https://www.amazon.ca/Rambler-Samuel-Johnson-ebook/dp/B006U9DDXG/, using the recommendation in Leighton that one Kindle "location" equals about 23 words.
- **available on YouTube** Benson, "Samuel Johnson."
- **us your Compliance** Johnson, *Letters*, vol. I, pp. 67–68; quoted in Boswell, *Life*, p. 199.
- **exalt their virtue** Johnson, *Yale*, vol. 2, *Idler and Adventurer*, pp. 471–472, http://www.yalejohnson.com/frontend/sda_viewer?n=107623.
- **sentences are brief** Johnson, *Yale*, vol. 2, *Idler and Adventurer*, pp. xv, xx, http://www.yalejohnson.com/frontend/sda_viewer?n=106843.
- **delighting each other** Johnson, *Yale*, vol. 2, *Idler and Adventurer*, p. 72, http://www.yalejohnson.com/frontend/sda_viewer?n=106843.
- **attend the funeral** Bundock, "Prime," p. 42.

- **have little relation** Johnson, *Yale*, vol. 1, *Diaries*, pp. 50, 127, http://www.yalejohnson.com/frontend/sda_viewer?n=106841; *Letters*, vol. I, p. 90 (quoted in Martin, p. 296).
- **return to Abissinia** Johnson, *Yale*, vol. 16, *Rasselas*, p. 176, http://www.yalejohnson.com/frontend/sda_viewer?n=106857.
- **to do well** Johnson, *Letters*, vol. I, pp. 174–177.
- **Sam was writing** *Encyclopedia of Language & Linguistics*, pp. 181–184.
- **princes' heroic campaigns** *Beowulf*, pp. 2–3.
- **cease to sleep** Johnson, *Dictionary Online*, "To wake. v.n.," sense 3, https://johnsonsdictionaryonline.com/1755/wake_vn.
- **an unornamented style** Seward, p. 343.
- **list of items** The best source for information about Sam's style, and from which I borrow heavily here, is Wimsatt, *Prose Style*.
- **and salutary remonstrances** Johnson, *Yale*, vol. 3, *The Rambler*, p. 220, http://www.yalejohnson.com/frontend/sda_viewer?n=106854.
- **or other limit** Fowler, pp. 130–131.
- **essays professedly serious** Johnson, *Yale*, vol. 5, *Rambler*, pp. 319–320, http://www.yalejohnson.com/frontend/sda_viewer?n=106856.

CHAPTER 6

- **in factions attending** Gorrie, *Gentle Riots?*; Gorrie, Telephone interview.
- **this is serialization** The first one was published in 1837. Dickens, *Pickwick Papers*, pp. vii–viii.
- **been very successful** Johnson, *Letters*, vol. I, p. 158.
- **what is obscure** Johnson, *Yale*, vol. 7, *Shakespeare*, p. 51, http://www.yalejohnson.com/frontend/sda_viewer?n=108481.
- **obscurity of Shakespeare** Johnson, *Yale*, vol. 7, *Shakespeare*, p. 54, http://www.yalejohnson.com/frontend/sda_viewer?n=108481.
- **rarities very communicative** Johnson, *Yale*, vol. 7, *Shakespeare*, p. 105, http://www.yalejohnson.com/frontend/sda_viewer?n=106858.
- **a Shakespearean editor** Stern.
- **objects very well** Hawkins, p. 444.

- **and their commentaries** Stern.
- **is apparently neglecting** Hawkins, p. 219.
- **somewhat paralysed him** Martin, p. 334.
- **by Sam. Johnson** Shakespeare, *Plays*, 1765.
- **are very insightful** See Martin, pp. 375–377.
- **as an editor** Johnson, *Yale*, vol. 7, *Shakespeare*, p. 704, http://www.yalejohnson.com/frontend/sda_viewer?n=106858.
- **are actually like** Stern.
- **instruct by pleasing** Johnson, *Yale*, vol. 7, *Shakespeare*, p. 67, http://www.yalejohnson.com/frontend/sda_viewer?n=106858.
- **moral in tow** Nabokov, *Lolita*, p. 314.
- **the dancing pun** Johnson, *Yale*, vol. 7, *Shakespeare*, p. 74, http://www.yalejohnson.com/frontend/sda_viewer?n=106858.
- **the way through** Johnson, *Yale*, vol. 7, *Shakespeare*, p. 83, http://www.yalejohnson.com/frontend/sda_viewer?n=106858.
- **only the first** Johnson, *Yale*, vol. 7, *Shakespeare*, p. 96, http://www.yalejohnson.com/frontend/sda_viewer?n=106858.
- **to criticize him** Johnson, *Yale*, vol. 7, *Shakespeare*, p. 96, http://www.yalejohnson.com/frontend/sda_viewer?n=106858.
- **are necessary evils** Johnson, *Yale*, vol. 7, *Shakespeare*, pp. 107, 111, http://www.yalejohnson.com/frontend/sda_viewer?n=106858.
- **and social neglect** Martin, p. 372.

CHAPTER 7

- **countrymen cannot help** Boswell, *Life*, pp. 269–270.
- **eating or drinking** Boswell, *Life*, p. 308.
- **mind anything else** Boswell, *Life*, p. 308.
- **sensations or ideas** Blackburn, "Berkeley, George (1685–1753) Irish Idealist."
- **refute it thus** Boswell, *Life*, p. 310.
- **any man alive** Boswell, *Life*, p. 106
- **is not illegal** Rosenthal, Telephone interview.
- **man of pleasure** See a digitized version of the 1787 edition on the Internet Archive at https://archive.org/details/harris-ladies-3, as well as a project by Matthew Sangster called *Romantic London* which maps the 1788 edition at http://www.romanticlondon.org/harris-list-1788/. And for more extensive

information about prostitution in the eighteenth century, see: Rosenthal, *Infamous*; Rosenthal, editor, *Nightwalkers*; and Lubey.

- **including this one** A lot has been written about Boswell's life in general and his relationship with Sam in particular. See Martin, *Boswell*; and Radner, *Johnson and Boswell*.
- **scarred by smallpox** Martin, p. 320.
- **in with Sam** Bundock, *Fortunes*, p. 53.
- **would be paid** Boulukos.
- **till the end** Martin, p. 516; Meyers, pp. 441–442.
- **be educated properly** Martin, p. 400.
- **totals over £2,000** Bundock, *Fortunes*, pp. 173–174.
- **pounds was scandalous** Nokes, p. 355.
- **the poor creature** Boswell, *Life*, p. 933; see also Piozzi, *Anecdotes*, 2nd. ed., p. 257.
- **House in London** Taylor.

CHAPTER 8

- **wholesome, green and rural** Thrale.
- **that he owns** Seccombe, p. 13.
- **occupy eighty-nine acres** Thrale.
- **lake and drawbridge** Seccombe, p. 13.
- **of the house** Thrale.
- **he turns 30** Piozzi, *Anecdotes*, 2nd ed., p. 125.
- **an honest man** Piozzi, *Anecdotes*, 2nd ed., p. 125.
- **in his life** Martin, p. 384.
- **in the morning** Piozzi, *Anecdotes*, 2nd ed., pp. 123–124.
- **one scholar writes** McCarthy, p. 26.
- **in his Face** Piozzi, *Thraliana*, vol. 1, p. 356.
- **April 4, 1781** Mary Hyde, pp. 52–54.
- **meal finished him** Wain, p. 354
- **early as 1740** Nokes, p. 86.
- **middle of nowhere** Martin, p. 124.
- **for Mrs. Johnson** Boswell, *Life*, p. 120.
- **my amorous propensities** Boswell, *Life*, p. 174.
- **excite my genitals** Martin, p. 245.
- **care in 1768** Quoted in Meyers, p. 360.
- **his wife's death** Balderston, pp. 11, 13.

- **manicis insana cogitatio** Johnson, *Yale*, vol. 1, *Diaries*, p. 140, http://www.yalejohnson.com/frontend/sda_viewer?n=106841.
- **foot-fetters and manacles** Meyers, pp. 360–365.
- **the Rod enough** Balderston, "Johnson's Vile Melancholy," pp. 5–7. For an account of these incidents outside of academic articles and biographies, see Gopnik.
- **his defecation schedule** Baldwin.
- **really up to** Greene, pp. 186, 191.
- **masochism theory discredited** Martin, p. 388.
- **achievement more impressive** Meyers, pp. 6–7.
- **thought a crime** Boswell, *Applause*, p. 112.
- **was sometimes overcome** Boswell, *Life*, p. 1048.
- **having good practice** Boswell, *Life*, p. 1048.
- **masturbation, chains and whips** Meyers, p. 438.

CHAPTER 9

- **of mainland Scotland** Leask.
- **horseback, foot and boat** Meyers, p. 370.
- **on the mainland** Wain, p. 307.
- **modes of travel** Page, pp. 41–50.
- **Ossian were fakes** Boswell, *Life*, p. 271.
- **extant Gaelic ballads** Curley, p. 2.
- **by any other** Johnson,*Yale*, vol. 9, *Journey*, p. 118, http://www.yalejohnson.com/frontend/sda_viewer?n=106844.
- **if you will** Johnson, *Letters*, vol. II, pp. 168–169; see also Stafford.

CHAPTER 10

- **the English poets** Boswell, *Life*, p. 639; Johnson, *Letters*, vol. III, p. 20.
- **to involve it** Johnson, *Yale*, vol. 22, *Lives*, p. 973, http://www.yalejohnson.com/frontend/sda_viewer?n=107694.
- **unlike anything else** Johnson, *Yale*, vol. 22, *Lives*, pp. 977–980, http://www.yalejohnson.com/frontend/sda_viewer?n=107694.
- **possible nor recommendable** Johnson, *Yale*, vol. 22, *Lives*, p. 984, http://www.yalejohnson.com/frontend/sda_viewer?n=107694.

- **considered as original** Johnson, *Yale*, vol. 22, *Lives*, p. 1023, http://www.yalejohnson.com/frontend/sda_viewer?n=107694.
- **survived the years** Johnson, *Letters*.
- **notice to patron** Johnson, *Yale*, vol. 6, *Poems*, p. 99, http://www.yalejohnson.com/frontend/sda_viewer?n=107813.
- **paid with flattery** Johnson, *Dictionary Online*, "Patron. n.s.," https://johnsonsdictionaryonline.com/1755/patron_ns.
- **grow much better** Johnson, *Letters*, vol. IV, p. 356.
- **by chronic bronchitis** Wiltshire, p. 40.
- **castor (plant) oil** See Johnson, *Letters*, vol. IV, pp. 351–436; Wiltshire, pp. 55–58.
- **servant, Sam.** Johnson, *Letters*, vol. IV, pp. 445–446.

CHAPTER 11

- **assigned to Sam** Page, p. 86.
- **back to London** Page, p. 88.
- **variety of disorders** Wiltshire, p. 50.
- **of his illness** Boswell, *Life*, p. 901.
- **specific medical qualifications** Savage, "'Cunning Folk.'"
- **quite a following** Savage, Telephone Interview.
- **to merit unrefin'd** Johnson, *Yale*, vol. 6, *Poems*, p. 314, http://www.yalejohnson.com/frontend/sda_viewer?n=107958.
- **he might see** Boswell, *Life*, p. 911; Johnson, *Letters*, vol. IV, pp. 49–50; both quoted in Page, p. 93.
- **of the Poets** Page, p. 94.
- **conversation and writing** Boswell, *Life*, p. 916.
- **on to talk** Boswell, *Life*, p. 306.
- **never was exhausted** Johnson, *Letters*, vol. IV, p. 200.
- **an interesting person** See the distinction in the *Oxford English Dictionary: OED*, senses II.2 and II.3.
- **to and preferred** Martin, p. 506.
- **of the heart** Page, p. 103.
- **conducive to health** Boswell, *Life*, p. 976.
- **by our Marriage** Quoted in McIntyre, p. 199.
- **your faithful Servt** Quoted in McIntyre, p. 199.
- **you permit it** Johnson, *Letters*, vol. IV, p. 338.
- **God bless you** The actual letter is part of a collection of Piozzi's correspondence held by Harvard University, and is

available online at https://iiif.lib.harvard.edu/manifests/view/drs:8439190$18i.

- **Sick Man's Journal** See Johnson, *Yale*, vol. 1, *Diaries*, pp. xviii–xix, for the editors' explanation of the context of this journal among others that Sam kept during his life (http://www.yalejohnson.com/frontend/sda_viewer?n=106841), as well as for the full text, pp. 371–417 (http://www.yalejohnson.com/frontend/sda_viewer?n=106858).
- **and discernible effects** Wiltshire, p. 58.
- **poorly and low** Hoole, Nov. 22, Dec. 3, Dec. 8.
- **reconciliation with God** Hawkins, p. 353.
- **of any present** Hoole, Dec. 13.
- **December 13, 1784** Martin, p. 522.

BIBLIOGRAPHY

Balderston, Katharine C. "Johnson's Vile Melancholy." *The Age of Johnson: Essays Presented to Chauncey Brewster Tinker*, edited by Frederick W. Hilles, New Haven: Yale University Press, 1949, pp. 3–14.

Baldwin, Barry. "The Mysterious Letter 'M' in Johnson's Diaries." *Age of Johnson*, 6, 1994, pp. 131–145.

Barclay, Katie. Personal interview with Wayne Jones. Ottawa, Canada. Oct. 3, 2019.

Benson, David. "Samuel Johnson: The Rambler Essays." *YouTube*, uploaded by David Benson, Oct. 5, 2020, https://www.youtube.com/playlist?list=PLUlWtsrjue1pWGOQHf4wYk-kng0avlWwh.

Beowulf: A New Verse Translation, by Seamus Heaney, New York: Norton, 2000.

The Bible. New International Version (NIV). *Bible Gateway*, https://www.biblegateway.com/versions/New-International-Version-NIV-Bible/.

Blackburn, Simon. *The Oxford Dictionary of Philosophy*. 3rd ed., Oxford: Oxford University Press, 2016.

Boswell, James. *Boswell: The Applause of the Jury, 1782–1785*, edited by Irma S. Lustig and Frederick A. Pottle, New York: McGraw-Hill, 1981.

Boswell, James. *Boswell's London Journal, 1762–1763*, edited by Frederick A. Pottle, London: Heinemann, 1950.

Boswell, James. *The Life of Samuel Johnson*, edited by David Womersley, London: Penguin Random House, 2008.

Boulukos, George. Email interview with Wayne Jones. Aug. 19, 2019.

Bundock, Michael. *The Fortunes of Francis Barber: The True Story of the Jamaican Slave Who Became Samuel Johnson's Heir*, New Haven: Yale University Press, 2015.

Bundock, Michael. "Prime." *The Oxford Handbook of Samuel Johnson*, edited by Jack Lynch, Oxford: Oxford University Press, 2022, pp. 31–48.

Burney, Fanny. *The Early Journals and Letters of Fanny Burney, 1774–1777*. Vol. 2, edited by Lars E. Troide, Montreal and Kingston: McGill-Queen's University Press, 1990.

Carlson, C. Lennart. *The First Magazine: A History of the Gentleman's Magazine, with an Account of Dr. Johnson's Editorial Activity and of the Notice Given America in the Magazine*, Providence: Brown University, 1938.

Cawdrey, Robert. *A Table Alphabeticall, Conteyning and Teaching the True Writing and Understanding of Hard Usuall English Wordes, Borrowed from the Hebrew, Greeke, Latine, or French, &c., with the Interpretation Thereof by Plaine English Words, Gathered for the Benefit & Helpe of Ladies, Gentlewomen, or Any Other Unskilfull Persons, Whereby They May the More Easilie and Better Understand*

Many Hard English Wordes, Which They Shall Heare or Read in Scriptures, Sermons, or Elswhere, and Also Be Made Able to Use the Same Aptly Themselves, London: Printed by I. R. for Edmund Weaver, 1604.

Chesterfield, Lord. Letter. *The World*, no. 100, Nov. 28, 1754, pp. 601–602, https://archive.org/details/sim_world-1753_1754-11-28_2_100/.

Clayton, Stephanie. Email interview with Wayne Jones. Sept. 22, 2019.

Clifford, James L. *Dictionary Johnson: Samuel Johnson's Middle Years*, New York: McGraw-Hill, 1979.

Clifford, James L. *Young Sam Johnson*, New York: McGraw-Hill, 1955.

Cotter, Colleen. Personal interview with Wayne Jones. London, England. Apr. 9, 2019.

Craven, Maxwell. Email to Wayne Jones. Dec. 23, 2021.

Curley, Thomas M. *Samuel Johnson, the Ossian Fraud, and the Celtic Revival in Great Britain and Ireland*, Cambridge: Cambridge University Press, 2009.

Davies, J. D. "Gerard, Charles, Second Earl of Macclesfield." *Oxford Dictionary of National Biography*, https://www.oxforddnb.com/.

De Bruyn, Frans. Telephone interview with Wayne Jones. Nov. 1, 2019.

Derbyshire. *Derbyshire Hearth Tax Assessments 1662–70*, edited by David G. Edwards, Chesterfield: Derbyshire Record Society, 1982.

Dickens, Charles. *The Pickwick Papers*, edited by James Kinsley, Oxford: Oxford University Press, 2008.

Doyle, Marjorie. Email interview with Wayne Jones. Oct. 19, 2019.

Dr Ben Jackson [@BenLTJackson]. "#Twitterstorians I am trying to find out when boys/young men got their first wigs in the long 18C (1650-1850 - yes I know its long!), anyone have any thoughts for reading/sources/references. Help a poor fourth year out! :)." *Twitter*, Apr. 21, 2020, https://twitter.com/BenLTJackson/status/1252537615749910533.

Encyclopedia of Language & Linguistics, 2nd ed., edited by Keith Brown, Amsterdam: Elsevier, 2006. 14 vols.

Fowler, H. W. *A Dictionary of Modern English Usage.* 1926, edited by David Crystal, Oxford: Oxford University Press, 2009.

The Gentleman's Magazine, vol. 8 (Nov. 1738), https://archive.org/details/s2492id1185811/page/580/mode/2up.

The Gentleman's Magazine: and Historical Chronicle, vol. 8 (Mar. 1738), https://archive.org/details/s2492id1185811/page/156/mode/2up.

The Gentleman's Magazine: or, Trader's Monthly Intelligencer, vol. 1 (Jan. 1731), https://www.gutenberg.org/files/53351/53351-h/53351-h.htm.

Gopnik, Adam. "Man of Fetters: Dr. Johnson and Mrs. Thrale," *The New Yorker*, Nov. 30, 2008, https://www.newyorker.com/magazine/2008/12/08/man-of-fetters.

Gorrie, Richard. *Gentle Riots? Theatre Riots in London, 1730–1780.* 2000. University of Guelph, PhD thesis, http://www.collectionscanada.gc.ca/obj/s4/f2/dsk3/ftp04/nq65823.pdf.

Gorrie, Richard. Telephone interview with Wayne Jones. Apr. 29, 2020.

Great Britain. Calendar (New Style) Act 1750, 23 & 24 Geo 2, http://www.legislation.gov.uk/apgb/Geo2/24/23.

Greene, Donald. "'A Secret Far Dearer to Him Than His Life': Johnson's 'Vile Melancholy' Reconsidered." *The Selected Essays of Donald Greene*, Lewisburg, PA: Bucknell University Press, 2004.

Harris's List of Covent-Garden Ladies, or Man of Pleasure's Kalendar, Containing the Histories and Some Curious Anecdotes of the Most Celebrated Ladies Now on the Town, or in Keeping, and Also of Many of Their Keepers, for the Year 1787, London: H. Ranger, 1787. *Internet Archive*, https://archive.org/details/harris-ladies-3.

Hawkins, John. *The Life of Samuel Johnson, LL.D.* 1787. Edited by O M Brack, Jr., Athens and London: University of Georgia Press, 2009.

Hessell, Nikki. *Literary Authors, Parliamentary Reporters: Johnson, Coleridge, Hazlitt, Dickens*, Cambridge: Cambridge University Press, 2012.

Holloway, Sally. *The Game of Love in Georgian England: Courtship, Emotions, and Material Culture*, Oxford: Oxford University Press, 2019.

Holmes, Richard. *Dr Johnson and Mr Savage*, London: Harper Perennial, 2005.

Hoole, John. *Journal Narrative Relative to Doctor Johnson's Last Illness Three Weeks Before His Death Kept by John Hoole, MDCCLXXXIV*. Edited by O M Brack, Iowa City: Windhover Press, 1972.

Hyde, Mary. *The Thrales of Streatham Park*, Cambridge: Harvard University Press, 1976.

Institute for Name-Studies, University of Nottingham. *Key to English Place-Names*, http://kepn.nottingham.ac.uk/.

Jamil, Miriam Al. "Printed Afterlives: Joshua Reynolds' 'Johnson Arguing' portrait, 1769," *Romantic Illustration Network Blog*, Feb. 23, 2022, https://romanticillustrationnetwork.com/2022/02/23/printed-afterlives-joshua-reynolds-johnson-arguing-portrait-1769/.

Johnson, Samuel. *Johnson's Dictionary: A Modern Selection*, edited by E. L. McAdam and George Milne, New York: Pantheon Books, 1963.

Johnson, Samuel. *Johnson's Dictionary Online*, https://johnsonsdictionaryonline.com/.

Johnson, Samuel. *The Letters of Samuel Johnson*, edited by Bruce Redford, Princeton, NJ: Princeton University Press, 1992. 5 vols.

Johnson, Samuel. *The Rambler*. 1750–1752. *The Yale Digital Edition of the* Works of Samuel Johnson, vols. 3, 4, and 5, edited by W. J. Bate and Albrecht B. Strauss, New Haven and London: Yale University Press, 1969, http://www.yalejohnson.com/frontend/sda_viewer?n=106854, http://www.yalejohnson.com/frontend/sda_viewer?n=106855, http://www.yalejohnson.com/frontend/sda_viewer?n=106856.

Johnson, Samuel. *Samuel Johnson, A Journey to the Western Islands of Scotland; James Boswell, The Journal of a Tour to the Hebrides*, edited by Peter Levi, London: Penguin, 1984.

Johnson, Samuel. *Samuel Johnson's Dictionary of the English Language 1756: Online Edition*, http://www.whichenglish.com/Johnsons-Dictionary/index.html.

Johnson, Samuel. *The Yale Digital Edition of the Works of Samuel Johnson*, New Haven and London: Yale University Press, http://www.yalejohnson.com/.

Johnston, Freya. "Savage, Richard." *Oxford Dictionary of National Biography*, https://www.oxforddnb.com/.

Jones, Wayne. *A Study of Johnson's Rambler.* 1982. University of Toronto, MA thesis, https://waynejones.ca/wp-content/uploads/Wayne_Jones_thesis_UToronto_1982.pdf.

Kaminski, Thomas. *The Early Career of Samuel Johnson*, New York: Oxford University Press, 1987.

Leask, Emma. "The Lure of the Hebrides," *New York Times*, Jan. 29, 2014, http://www.nytimes.com/2014/01/30/greathomesanddestinations/the-lure-of-the-hebrides.html.

Leighton, Jennifer. "What Does Location Mean on a Kindle?" *Techwalla*, https://www.techwalla.com/articles/what-does-location-mean-on-a-kindle.

Lichfield City Council. "Civic Insignia," https://www.lichfield.gov.uk/Civic_Insignia_684.aspx.

Lichfield City Council. "History of Lichfield," https://www.lichfield.gov.uk/History_of_Lichfield_694.aspx.

Lichfield City Council. "Statistics," [2011], https://web.archive.org/web/20110724162428/http://www.lichfield.gov.uk/cc-statistics.ihtml.

"Lichfield: The Place and Street Names, Population and Boundaries." *A History of the County of Stafford: Volume 14, Lichfield*, edited by M. W. Greenslade, London: Victoria County History, 1990, *British History Online*, Jan. 23, 2023, pp. 37–42, http://www.british-history.ac.uk/vch/staffs/vol14/pp37-42.

Lubey, Kathleen. *What Pornography Knows: Sex and Social Protest since the Eighteenth Century*, Stanford: Stanford University Press, 2022.

Lynch, Jack. "Samuel Johnson and the 'First English Dictionary.'" *The Cambridge Companion to English Dictionaries*, edited by Sarah Ogilvie, Cambridge, UK: Cambridge University Press, 2020, pp. 142–153.

Martin, Peter. *A Life of James Boswell*, New Haven and London: Yale University Press, 2000.

Martin, Peter. *Samuel Johnson: A Biography*, London: Phoenix, 2009.

McCarthy, William. *Hester Thrale Piozzi: Portrait of a Literary Woman*, Chapel Hill and London: University of North Carolina Press, 1985.

McConchie, Roderick W. "Cawdrey, Coote, and 'Hard Vsual English Wordes.'" *The Cambridge Companion to English Dictionaries*, edited by Sarah Ogilvie, Cambridge: Cambridge University Press, 2020, pp. 103–113.

McIntyre, Ian. *Hester: The Remarkable Life of Dr Johnson's "Dear Mistress,"* London: Constable, 2008.

Meyers, Jeffrey. *Samuel Johnson: The Struggle*, New York: Basic Books, 2008.

Mills, A. D. *A Dictionary of British Place Names*, Oxford: Oxford University Press, 2011.

Murray, T. J. "Dr Samuel Johnson's Movement Disorder," *British Medical Journal,* vol. 1, June 16, 1979, pp. 1610–1614.

Nabokov, Vladimir. *Lolita.* 1955. New York: Vintage International, 1989.

Nabokov, Vladimir. *Selected Letters 1940–1977*, San Diego: Harcourt Brace Jovanovich, 1989.

National Archives. *Currency Converter: 1270–2017*, https://www.nationalarchives.gov.uk/currency/.

Nokes, David. *Samuel Johnson: A Life*, New York: Henry Holt, 2009.

Official Data Foundation. *Inflation Calculator*, https://www.officialdata.org/.

O'Flaherty, Patrick. "Towards an Understanding of Johnson's *Rambler*," *Studies in English Literature, 1500–1900*, vol. 18, no. 3, summer 1978, pp. 523–536.

Olsen, Kirstin. *Daily Life in 18th-Century England*, Westport, CT: Greenwood, 1999.

Oxford Concise Medical Dictionary, 10th ed., edited by Elizabeth A. Martin and Jonathan Law, Oxford: Oxford University Press, 2020.

Oxford English Dictionary: OED, Oxford: Oxford University Press, 2023, https://www.oed.com/.

Page, Norman. *A Dr Johnson Chronology*, Basingstoke and London: Macmillan, 1990.

Peifer, Karl-Nikolaus. "The Return of the Commons— Copyright History as a Common Source." *Privilege and Property: Essays on the History of Copyright*, edited by Ronan Deazley, Martin Kretschmer, and Lionel Bently, Cambridge: Open Book Publishers, 2010, pp. 347–357.

Piozzi, Hester Lynch Thrale. *Anecdotes of the Late Samuel Johnson, LL.D. During the Last Twenty Years of His Life*, London: T. Cadell, 1786, [1st ed.], https://babel.hathitrust.org/cgi/pt?id=nyp.33433082380795.

Piozzi, Hester Lynch Thrale. *Anecdotes of the Late Samuel Johnson, LL.D. During the Last Twenty Years of His Life*, London: T. Cadell, 1786, 2nd ed., https://babel.hathitrust.org/cgi/pt?id=uc1.31822038198909.

Piozzi, Hester Lynch Thrale. *Thraliana: The Diary of Mrs. Hester Lynch Thrale (Later Mrs. Piozzi), 1776–1809*, edited by Katharine C. Balderston, Oxford: Clarendon Press, 1942. 2 vols.

Porter, Roy. *English Society in the Eighteenth Century*, revised ed., London: Penguin Books, 1991.

Radner, John B. *Johnson and Boswell: A Biography of Friendship*, New Haven, CT: Yale University Press, 2012.

Raven, James. "James Raven: Interview." Conducted by James Rivington, *British Academy Review*, vol. 36, Dec. 19, 2019, https://www.thebritishacademy.ac.uk/publishing/review/36/british-academy-review-36-james-raven-interview/.

Read, Allen Walker. "The Beginnings of English Lexicography." *Dictionaries* 24 (2003), pp. 187–226, https://doi.org/10.1353/dic.2003.0010.

Reade, Aleyn Lyell. *Johnsonian Gleanings*, London: Privately Printed for the Author by Percy Lund, Humphries & Co., 1909–1952, https://archive.org/search.php?query=%22johnsonian+gleanings%22. 10 parts.

Reddick, Allen. *The Making of Johnson's Dictionary, 1746–1773*, Cambridge: Cambridge University Press, 1990.

Reynolds, Frances. "Recollections of Dr. Johnson." *Johnsonian Miscellanies*, arranged and edited by James Birkbeck Hill, New York: Harper, 1897, vol. 2, pp. 250–300, https://hdl.handle.net/2027/coo.31924012961714.

Rogers, Samuel. *Reminiscences and Table-talk of Samuel Rogers, Banker, Poet, & Patron of the Arts, 1763–1855*, London: R. Brimley Johnson, 1903, https://archive.org/details/reminiscencestab00rogeiala/mode/2up.

Rosenthal, Laura J. *Infamous Commerce: Prostitution in Eighteenth-Century British Literature and Culture*, Ithaca, NY: Cornell University Press, 2006.

Rosenthal, Laura J., editor. *Nightwalkers: Prostitute Narratives from the Eighteenth Century*, Peterborough, ON: Broadview Press, 2008.

Rosenthal, Laura J. Telephone interview with Wayne Jones. Sept. 13, 2019.

Sangster, Matthew. "Mapping Harris's List of Covent-Garden Ladies (1788)," *Romantic London*, http://www.romanticlondon.org/harris-list-1788/.

Savage, William. "'Cunning Folk': Witchcraft, Healing and Superstition," *Pen and Pension*, Nov. 29, 2017, https://penandpension.com/2017/11/29/cunning-folk-witchcraft-healing-and-superstition/.

Savage, William. "The Georgian Way with Debt," *Pen and Pension*, July 19, 2017, https://penandpension.com/2017/07/19/the-georgian-way-with-debt/.

Savage, William. Telephone interview with Wayne Jones. Sept. 6, 2019.

Seccombe, Thomas. "Essay Introductory." *Doctor Johnson and Mrs Thrale, Including Mrs Thrale's Journal of the Welsh Tour Made in 1774 and Much Hitherto Unpublished Correspondence of the Streatham Coterie*, by A. M. Broadley, London and New York: John Lane, 1910, pp. 3–77.

Seward, Anna. "Anna Seward on Johnson's Prose Style." *Samuel Johnson: The Critical Heritage*, edited by James T. Boulton, London: Routledge, 1996, pp. 343–344, https://doi-org.proxy.library.carleton.ca/10.4324/9780203197356.

Shakespeare, William. *The Plays of William Shakespeare in Eight Volumes, with the Corrections and Illustrations of Various Commentators, to Which Are Added Notes by Sam. Johnson*, London: J. and R. Tonson [et al.], 1765. 8 vols.

Shakespeare, William. *The Plays of William Shakespeare in Ten Volumes, with the Corrections and Illustrations of Various Commentators, to Which Are Also Added Notes by Samuel Johnson and George Steevens*, 2nd ed., London: C. Bathurst [et al.], 1778. 10 vols.

Sherbo, Arthur. "Brett [*née* Mason], Anne [*other married name* Anne Gerard, countess of Macclesfield]." *Oxford Dictionary of National Biography*, https://www.oxforddnb.com/.

Simpson, John. "The First Dictionaries of English," *OED Blog*, Apr. 16, 2012, https://public.oed.com/blog/the-first-dictionaries-of-english/.

St Werburgh's Church. *St Werburgh's Derby*, "Our Story," https://stwderby.org/story.

Stafford, Fiona. "Dr Johnson and the Ruffian: New Evidence in the Dispute between Samuel Johnson and James Macpherson," *Notes & Queries*, vol. 36, no. 1, 1989, pp. 70–77.

Statista. "Purchasing Power of One British Pound Sterling (GBP) from 1209 to 2019," https://www.statista.com/statistics/1031884/value-pound-sterling-since/.

Stern, Tiffany. Personal interview with Wayne Jones. Oxford, England. Apr. 8, 2019.

Swift, Jonathan. *A Proposal for Correcting, Improving and Ascertaining the English Tongue, in a Letter to the Most Honourable Robert, Earl of Oxford and Mortimer, Lord High Treasurer of Great Britain.* 2nd ed., London: Benj. Tooke, 1712, https://jacklynch.net/Texts/proposal.html.

Tankard, Paul. "'Try to Resolve Again': Johnson and the Written Art of Everyday Life." *New Essays on Samuel Johnson: Revaluation*, edited by Anthony W. Lee, Newark: University of Delaware Press, 2018, pp. 217–234.

Taylor, Penny. "A History of Hodge," *The Samuel Johnson Birthplace Museum Blog*, Aug. 8, 2019, https://sjmuseum.wordpress.com/2019/08/08/a-history-of-hodge/.

Thorne, Tony. Telephone interview with Wayne Jones. Oct. 7, 2019.

Thrale, David. "Streatham Park," *Thrale.com*, Sept. 26, 2009, http://www.thrale.com/streatham_park.

UK Office for National Statistics. "Phase One: Census 2021 First Results," https://census.gov.uk/census-2021-results/phase-one-first-results.

Vickers, Ilse. "Dr Johnson and Dr Jung: Two Physicians of the Soul. Part II: Johnson's Troubled Faith," *The New Rambler*, 20, 2016/2017, pp. 10–17.

Virgil. *The Aeneid, the Eclogues, and the Georgics in English and Latin*, Halcyon Press, 2010.

Wain, John. *Samuel Johnson*, New York: Viking, 1975.

Webster, Noah. *A Compendious Dictionary of the English Language, in which Five Thousand Words Are Added to the Number Found in the Best English*

Compends; the Orthography Is, in Some Instances, Corrected; the Pronunciation Marked by an Accent or Other Suitable Direction; and the Definition of Many Words Amended and Improved, New Haven: Stoney's Press, 1806, https://archive.org/details/compendiousdictionaryoftheenglishlanguage1806/.

White, Jerry. "The Debtors' Prison in Samuel Johnson's London," *The New Rambler*, 2016–2017, pp. 45–52.

White, Jerry. *London in the Eighteenth Century: A Great and Monstrous Thing*, London: Bodley Head, 2012.

Wilson, Joanne. Telephone interview with Wayne Jones. Feb. 4, 2020.

Wiltshire, John. *Samuel Johnson in the Medical World: The Doctor and the Patient*, Cambridge: Cambridge University Press, 1991.

Wimsatt, W. K., Jr. *The Prose Style of Samuel Johnson*, New Haven, CT: Yale University Press, 1941.

ABOUT THE AUTHOR

WAYNE JONES IS A WRITER, editor, and podcaster in Ottawa, Canada, and a former academic librarian. He is the author of the novel *The Killing Type*, as well as a book about personal minimalism called *Less and Less*. Wayne is co-author of the biography *Greg Giraldo: A Comedian's Story*. His podcast is called *Writing & Editing*. For more information, see WayneJones.ca.